"I have observed how the grip of materialism can strangle a person and an organization. The only cure is understanding and applying God's principles of stewardship and generosity. It's all there in the Bible. Money DOES Matter. Learn from Mike, one of the best teachers of our time, how to get in sync with God's game plan."

—Bob Buford, Founding Chairman, Leadership Network

Other Books by Michael Slaughter

Spiritual Entrepreneurs: Six Principles for Risking Renewal (Abingdon Press, 1995)

Out on the Edge: A Wakeup Call for Church Leaders on the Edge of the Media Reformation (Abingdon Press, 1998)

Real Followers: Beyond Virtual Christianity (Abingdon Press, 1999)

UnLearning Church: Transforming Spiritual Leadership for the Emerging Church (Group, 2002)

Momentum for Life: Sustaining Personal Health, Integrity, and Strategic Focus as a Leader (Abingdon Press, 2005)

MONEY MATTERS

Financial Freedom for All God's Churches

Michael Slaughter

with

Kim Miller

Abingdon Press

Nashville

This book is printed on acid-free paper.

Unless otherwise noted, Scripture references are from *The Holy Bible: Today's New International Version* (TNIV), © 2001, 2005 by The International Bible Society. Used by permission.

Scripture references marked NRSV are from *The New Revised Standard Version*, © 1989 by The National Council of Churches of Christ. Used by permission.

09 10 11 12 13 14 15—11 10 09 08 07 06 05 04 03

This book is dedicated to the faithful stewards of

Ginghamsburg Church who are faithfully practicing

the disciplines of financial freedom for the

purpose of courageously serving

the needs of the world that God loves.

Acknowledgements

I thank:

My wife Carolyn for being a model of faithful stewardship and sacrifice in serving the needs of others in the mission of Jesus Christ.

Kim Miller (Creative Director of Ginghamsburg Church) for her incredible gift of making my work better.

My editor Paul Franklyn and his team at Abingdon Press for encouraging this project that I might not have otherwise written.

The people of Ginghamsburg Church who powerfully demonstrate the presence and power of Jesus through sacrificial giving and servant living.

Contents

*Samples of everything needed to implement
your church's strategic stewardship program**

1. Chief Stewardship Officer Annual Timeline
2. Kingdom Investor Hors d'oeuvres Initial Invitation
3. Kingdom Investor Dinner Invitation and RSVP
4. Kingdom Investor Dinner Invitation to Staff and RSVP
5. Kingdom Investor Invitation to Leadership Board
6. Annual Kingdom Investor Report: Hors d'oeuvres and Dinner
7. Board Member Follow-up Phone Call Script to Top Givers
8. Letter to All Active Givers
9. Commitment Card
10. Letter to Active Givers Who Did Not Return Commitment Card
11. Monthly Mission Update Letter
12. Monthly Kingdom Investor Letter

*Source files with art are on the DVD. Source copy for timeline and all letters are on the DVD in a folder that can be viewed on a computer with a DVD drive. The source file for a poster is also on the DVD. This poster can be modified and displayed at your church.

Foreword

Each year as the Christmas season draws near, I am reminded that Christmas is not my birthday—it's Jesus' birthday! The true Light that came into the world to bring hope and liberation to all people continues to shine brightly through real followers today. As disciples of Jesus, we are his hands and feet to take justice and hope to the lost and oppressed.

Materialism and debt continue to be one of the major oppressive forces that keep people from living fully as sons and daughters of God. We are created in the image of God and are never closer to God than when meeting the real needs of people. "Truly I tell you, whatever you did for one of the least of these brothers and sisters of mine, you did for me" (Matthew 25:40). My prayer is for you and your church to know the joy of financial freedom and the amazing abundance of generous living.

Mike Slaughter

January 2006

Chapter One

Let's Talk About Money: Jesus Did!

Let's face it: Money Matters! Whether we are perusing the shelves at the local bookstore, checking out the titles online, or watching Suze Orman give an hour-long discourse on cable TV, it soon becomes apparent that financial freedom is a huge felt need in our culture today. Sooner or later all God's children realize that money is a vital component of nearly every life-initiative. Sooner or later all God's churches realize that money is a vital component of nearly every mission initiative.

As I advise pastors from all over the country, I hear a prevailing myth that I believe has influenced the Church's approach to stewardship. It's a false perception that people stay away from church because of too much talk about money. Over a five-year period, however, our annual stewardship series at Ginghamsburg Church is now one of the highest-attended months of the year. This shift in our attendance patterns caused me to realize that people are not turned off because we are talking about money in the church. People are turned off because we are not connecting our money-talk to the relevant financial issues of their money-walk.

Since Jesus intentionally talked so much about money, the Church ought to be having the same conversations.

Jesus spoke often about money and the human felt need of freedom. Sixteen of Jesus' thirty-eight recorded parables deal with our attitudes and responsibilities toward money and possessions. Since Jesus intentionally talked so much about money, the Church ought to be having the same conversations.

People from every walk of life are absorbed in money matters. (Watch: "What's *Your* Money Matter?" on the companion DVD in this book.) Our issues range from exponential increases in fuel and health care costs to flattened incomes and cutbacks in wages and benefits. The US airline and automobile industries struggle to stay competitive in a global market, while men and women live with the economic uncertainties of their futures.

Younger adults ask critical questions: How can I make it on a single parent's income when daycare takes almost half of what I make? How will we pay for our children's college education? Will we ever be able to afford a home of our own? Can we still meet all of our obligations on our two incomes?

Older adults have more mature versions of the same fear-filled questions: Will my company's retirement plan, Social Security, or 401K be there for me when

I need it? How will we live on just one or a fixed income? What happens if I get sick and can no longer maintain employment?

Americans on every level are trying their best to stretch a dollar. What a tremendous opportunity for the Church to connect to people's real needs and become a valued source of wise counsel.

A second myth I find prevalent among pastors is that churched people plainly don't like to give. Conversely, contributions on behalf of the Asian Tsunami of 2004 and the Gulf Coast hurricanes of 2005 tell another story, a demonstration of the great outpouring of generosity that resides in the heart of the human spirit. Millions of dollars came from the private sector. The people of my congregation gave nearly one million dollars towards hunger and crisis relief in these situations, and we are not a congregation of wealthy people. Our people, like the people in your congregation, are created in the image of God's nature, which includes generosity in the face of need. "For God so loved the world that he *gave* his one and only Son" (John 3:16).

Our people, like the people in your congregation, are created in the image of God's nature, which includes generosity in the face of need.

Folks simply want to know that their giving is going to make a true difference. While it's true that most people are not energized by the thought of shoring up struggling church budgets, nearly all God's children deeply desire to make a significant contribution to an heroic cause.

In the fall of 2004, I read about the escalating atrocities in Darfur, Sudan. "Why do people continue to be so passive in the face of genocide?" I asked, unable to purge this nagging question from my spirit. "Why do God's people continue to acquiesce to genocide?" From the Holocaust to Bosnia, from Rwanda to the current crisis in Sudan, the Church has too often maintained silence in the face of evil.

Several weeks before Christmas that fall I turned those nagging questions into a quest. I asked the people of our congregation to spend only half as much on Christmas presents as expected, and to offer up the other half of their Christmas gifting money to the hunger crises in Sudan. "Christmas is Jesus' birthday," I reminded the people. "Celebrate your birthday on your birthday, but give Jesus something that would please Jesus on his birthday." At the same time I felt the intuitive voice of the Spirit within

"Christmas is Jesus' birthday," I reminded the people. "Celebrate your birthday on your birthday, but give Jesus something that would please Jesus on his birthday."

advising me not to announce the year-end church budget needs from the pulpit (as was our standard practice) but to keep lifting up the Sudan Miracle Offering on a weekly basis. The result was a Christmas week miracle offering of $327,000. This amount was enough to put 5000 displaced Darfurian families back into the farming business. Even more amazing is that our year-end budgetary need was oversubscribed! People deeply want the opportunity to make a heroic contribution.

Pastor Don Heatley and his people at Vision Faith Community Church in Warwick, New York, heard of our Sudan offering challenge. Their mission-focused congregation of 100 people raised $7000 to be used to keep children alive and safe in Darfur. The 200 faithful Jesus followers from Grace Lutheran Church in Corvallis, Oregon, brought $45,000. Money follows mission, not tired church budgets!

If our people show generosity in the face of great need, then why do the same men and women show such inconsistency in the practice of systematic, sacrificial stewardship? To inspire people toward faithful stewardship, church leaders must first understand the issues at hand. The reality is that materialism is embedded as a root in our lives, resulting in deep and paralyzing debt. Persons in our congregations struggle with giving, not because they don't want to give but because they are so over their heads in debt that they can't afford to give. Baby boomers are facing the reality of a retirement for which they haven't saved. The number of companies supplying fixed-rate pensions has dropped to under 20 percent ("Retirement: Ready or Not?" cnnmoney.com, March 1, 2006).

The reality of an overburdened Social Security system and the uncertainty of a post 9/11 stock market leave even the "financially secure" wondering about their future wellbeing. Americans between 25 and 34 hold the second highest rate of bankruptcy. During the 1990s college costs soared by an average of 38 percent. By the end of the decade almost two-thirds of students had borrowed money. The average college graduate owes $20,000 in student loans ("Why Young Americans Are Drowning In Debt," CSMonitor.com/content/collegeandfamily/moneyinyour205/p101676.asp). This doesn't count the credit card debt that the graduates accumulated during the four years away from home. The average 18 year-old college freshman is ill equipped to deal with the alluring enticement of the credit card companies who are waiting to meet them at every turn. Americans are maxing out their credit cards, facing record high college loans, and dealing with stagnant wages in a tight job market that is characterized by downsizing and outsourcing.

Let's face it, money matters—and the Church ought to be talking about it!

A Matter of the Heart

"For where your treasure is, there your heart will be also"
(Luke 12:34)

Money and our attitudes towards possessions are at the root a spiritual issue. Our fiscal behavior patterns betray our ultimate values and allegiances. Jesus said that we can't serve both God and money.

Our fiscal behavior patterns betray our ultimate values and allegiances. Faith has everything to do with our worldview. As I explained in the book, *Momentum for Life* (pg. 53-59), a worldview is a set of fundamental beliefs that determine our primary life values, decisions, and actions. Your worldview can have more to do with your values than your religion. Your worldview sets the course of your life action. A worldview determines everything from your sexual mores to your political persuasions.

The worldview that is most prevalent among our church attendees is soft secular. People with a soft secular worldview believe in God, but they place their trust in and draw their values from secular culture. They may profess Jesus but trust their own abilities, financial resources, and material possessions to provide meaning and security, rather than trusting God's promise of provision. It is difficult for soft secular people to make significant time or financial commitments to their churches. They believe in God, but God is not their first priority or passion. They live comfortably in two spheres, sacred and secular, but when pressed for time their default always goes to the secular. They bring Jesus into their worldview instead of being converted into his.

Many in my generation were raised to believe, "You can have it all!" We relished in the marketing mantra, "Have it your way." Many in my generation were raised to believe, "You can have it all!" We relished the marketing mantra, "Have it your way." Ours was the generation of excess and conspicuous consumption. We were the hippies of the 1960s and 1970s that became the BMW yuppies of the 1980s. In an age of global warming and diminishing fuel resources we require massive SUVs with $4000 wheel covers designed to handle the rigors of mountainous terrain. We never venture beyond the asphalt pavement that takes us to work, shop, and an occasional night out. Motorcycles, RV's, vacations, and luxury cruises we can't afford have created debt-encumbered lifestyles. We have raised a generation of children with a worldview that is centered in expressive individualism. "It's true if it works for me," they believe. "The experience found in *today* is all that matters." Generation X and the Millennial generation are seeking life's meaning in experience. The present is all that matters, and anything in the past or distant future is irrelevant to the expression of self and truth. Commitments made today, from the spoken "I do" of marriage, to the written signature on the credit card receipt, are viewed from the perspective of "my current experience."

Jesus tells the story in the Gospel of Luke of a wealthy entrepreneur who seeks meaning from money. When we buy into the lie that life is found in our ability to accumulate money and possessions, we find ourselves running after a waterless mirage, a lifeless source of counterfeit purpose.

> *A rich man had a fertile farm that produced fine crops. He said to himself, "What shall I do? I have no place to store my crops." Then he said, "This is what I'll do. I'll tear down my barns and build bigger ones, and there I will store my surplus grain. And I'll say to myself, 'You have plenty of grain laid up for many years. Take life easy; eat, drink and be merry!'"* (Luke 12:16-19).

Life is found in our ability to make a lasting contribution to the redemptive work of God in the world.

You know what happened next? The man turned around and died. He missed life! Life is found in our ability to make a lasting contribution to the redemptive work of God in the world. The only thing that lives beyond us is what we do for others in Jesus' name. *"You fool! This very night your life will be demanded from you. Then who will get what you have prepared for yourself?"* (v. 20).

The worst kind of fool is the one who believes that God exists but lives as if God's directives are not to be taken seriously.

Most of our churched people have bought into a malignant model of success. They measure their lives and values in terms of possessions, positions, and prestige. They pursue money over meaning and wealth over making a lasting life contribution. The worst kind of fool is the one who believes that God exists but lives as if God's directives are not to be taken seriously. *"This is how it will be with those who store up things for themselves but are not rich toward God"* (v. 21).

Financial Freedom

True abundance is found in the freedom that transpires from contributing to the wellbeing of another human being. Jesus reminds us, *"It is more blessed to give than to receive"* (Acts 20:35). Giving is the ultimate expression of our love for God and the means through which we discover a personal, life-long purpose. We are never closer to Jesus than we are when we are serving the needs of people.

> For I was hungry and you gave me something to eat, I was thirsty and you gave me something to drink, I was a stranger and you invited me in. I needed clothes and you clothed me, I was sick and you looked after me, I was in prison and you came to visit me.... Truly I tell you, whatever you **Jesus did not come to build** did for one of the least of these brothers **institutional agendas but to** and sisters of mine, you did for me" **liberate oppressed people.** (Matthew 25:35-40).

The primary mission of stewardship is one of liberation. Our people must discover the power of the freedom that comes through the disciplines of sound biblical financial principles. It is the priority of Jesus to free people, not to buttress budgets! Jesus did not come to build institutional agendas but to liberate oppressed people. Jesus frees us from the counterfeit gods of materialism and self so that we can experience true freedom and abundant life. Freedom gets a chance as we begin to see life through the lens of contribution rather than consumption; by connecting our lives to God's dreams rather than to greed-induced debt.

The first step is to change our life focus from self to service, from getting to giving. The second step is to deal with the oppressive burden of debt. People are not turned off because we are talking about money in the church. People are turned off because, as pastors, we aren't connecting our money-talk to their money-walk. Let's get started talking about money matters for all God's churches, by connecting to the issues of financial freedom for all God's children. *"The Spirit of the Lord is upon me, for he has anointed me to bring Good News to the poor. He has sent me to proclaim that captives be released, that the blind will see, that the oppressed will be set free, and that the time of the Load's favor has come"* (Luke 4:18).

Chapter Two

Speaking to the Felt Need: Freedom

"More than 5,100 file petitions for bankruptcy in just 2 days."

"Delphi Corporation's declaration of bankruptcy could close four of the five local area plants."

"Delta airlines laying off 1000 local area employees."

"Winter fuel costs will soar 30-70% over last year."

"Credit cards hike payments."

The headlines above recently graced the front page of our local newspaper, the *Dayton Daily News*. In this climate of growing concern I've noted the varied reactions of people in the community. Some appear fearful and panicked; others are functioning in a state of denial. A third group claims to be prepared for any possible scenario because of their training in life and faith, by practicing sound, biblical, money management principles.

Regardless of the state of our financial health, most of us wonder, "How on earth can we continue to stretch a dollar when costs are climbing at a faster rate than our income?" On top of the unknown variables of fuel costs and employment security emerge the federal guidelines that force Americans to pay more than the minimum against their credit card debt. The smallest

The Church, and more importantly its leadership, has a strategic opportunity and obligation to offer people the hope that can only be realized through the disciplined practice of sound financial stewardship principles.

amount that consumers can pay on their credit card debt could double. Under the rules, cardholders must pay enough to reduce the loan's principal and not just the cost of monthly interest.

Many of the people in our churches and communities have routinely made debt commitments with the intention of making only the minimum monthly payment. Suddenly they are thrust into a financial tailspin because they must reduce their debt and not maintain it. Feelings run the gamut: helplessness, fear, panic, apprehension, and emotional paralysis. The Church, and more importantly its leadership, has a strategic opportunity and obligation to offer people the hope that can only be realized through the disciplined practice of sound financial stewardship principles.

Our goal in developing this stewardship resource is to support you as a leader in your congregation, as you work through a comprehensive stewardship strategy that develops your people in three dimensions of their lives: The Focus of Heart Devotion, The Commitment to Debt Free Living, and The Practice of a Disciplined Lifestyle.*

The Focus of Heart Devotion

One night Jesus was approached by a man who had a burning life issue, a question that validated Jesus' conviction that all money matters are truly matters of the heart. The story from Matthew 19:16-24 features a rich young ruler who painfully turned away from Jesus because of his distorted focus of devotion. *"You can't serve God and money,"* he was told. If you serve and obey God first, aligning your lifestyle and fiscal patterns with God's directive, your money and possessions will serve you.

The young man wanted to have the all the rewards of heaven along with the security and power of worldly wealth. He believed in God but trusted his goods.

But if you put money first, you will end up becoming a slave to it. The young man wanted to have the all the rewards of heaven along with the security and power of worldly wealth. He believed in God but trusted his goods. His dependence on possessions and wealth for security and meaning smacked in the face of the love and provision of a heavenly parent.

Can you identify the man's felt need in his initial encounter with Jesus? Can you understand his innermost concerns? He wasn't asking Jesus about a great strategy that would yield a higher return on his investments. He was authentically concerned with the weightier issues of life—eternal life! Eternal life is about quality of life. This climbing young executive felt a deep need to experience life that was rooted in something more substantial than the quan-

Money and the things that we can purchase with money never fill the deeper places of the human soul. We are created to find that ultimate satisfaction in that which is eternal.

* Outlines of coinciding messages, "Devotion," Debt-free" and "Discipline" are featured in Chapter 4 of this book.

tity of possessions. Money and the things it acquires never fill the deeper places of the human soul. We are created to find that ultimate satisfaction in that which is eternal. *"If you want to be perfect,"* Jesus said, *"Go sell your possessions and give to the poor, and you will have treasure in heaven. Then come, follow me"* (Matthew 19:21).

Perfect means complete. Salvation affects every area of our lives. God doesn't "save" us just so we can go to heaven. Many people are going to go to heaven, but they are living on the rations of hell. They are missing the abundance that Jesus brings into their relationships with God and others. They may live in houses crammed full of things but know nothing of a home filled with **Many people are going to go to heaven, but they are living on the rations of hell.** contentment, love, and reverence for God's gracious gift of life. Their garages may be filled with all that glitters and gleams, but they will never have the opportunity to serve and contribute to the needs of others. Many people ask, "If I have Jesus in my life, why am I not experiencing his blessings?" You may not be experiencing God's blessings because you are not submitting your life to God's disciplines and direction. The young man who came to Jesus believed in Jesus, but came asking for the blessing of eternal life. Many people today believe in Jesus, but the objects of their devotion are the idols that they build or acquire with their hands.

Note the cause and effect relationship between disciplined devotion and financial freedom. *"If you fully obey the LORD your God and carefully follow all his commands I give you today, the LORD your God will set you high above all the nations on earth"* (Deuteronomy 28:1). The directive doesn't say *If you sometimes obey the LORD, your God*, but rather, *"If you fully … and carefully follow all his commands."* The Scripture qualifies the results of obedient devotion, *"All of these blessings will come on you and accompany you if you obey the Lord your God"* (v. 2). The promise is not for some of the blessings but all of the blessings! Your towns and fields will be blessed. Your family and work will prosper for God's

purpose. *"You will be blessed when you come in and when you go out"* (v .6). *"The Lord will open the heavens, the storehouse of his bounty, to send rain on your land in season and to bless all the work of your hands"* (v. 12).

What about the suffocating burden of debt? *"You will lend to many nations but will borrow from none"* (v.12). The list of blessings continues: *"The Lord will conquer your enemies when they attack you. They will attack you from one direction, but they will scatter from you in seven."* The Lord will guarantee a blessing on everything you do, everywhere you go! God has promised to *"fill your storehouses with grain."* Our only responsibility is to keep our devotion undiluted and undistracted; to seek first the Kingdom of God and God's righteousness! (Matthew 6:33).

God's blessings are the positive consequence of disciplined obedient devotion. Financial freedom necessitates going beyond the desire for fulfillment in all areas of life to the obedient actions that lead to that fulfillment. To get to the heart of fiscal freedom means that you must let go of materialistic addictions and idols and trust your wellbeing to the promise of God's love and provision. *"If you want to be perfect* [complete]," Jesus reminds the young man, *"go, sell your possessions and give to the poor, and you will have treasure in heaven. Then come, follow me"* (v. 21).

> **Our only responsibility is to keep our devotion undiluted and undistracted; to seek first the Kingdom of God and God's righteousness!**

The young man believes in God, but he is drawing his security and meaning from his money and possessions. If you truly want to be free then you must be willing to let go and release your possessions to the hand of God. As long as I keep my hand tightly clinched around my credit cards and money, then my faith is placed in plastic and cash instead of in the One who promises to meet my every need. The issue of devotion is a trust issue. By failing to release our money matters into God's hand we are saying in effect, "God, I don't trust you with this area of my life. I feel that I can do a better job of managing my resources than you can."

Control at its root is motivated by fear. What would it mean to truly let go and obediently order our money matters by God's purpose?

> **What would it mean to truly let go and obediently order our money matters by God's purpose?**

The newspaper headlines from the opening paragraph of this chapter are enough to invoke fear and uncertainty, even in the hearts of people of faith, even among church leaders who have watched as their communities lost manufacturing plants or farms. Fear paralyzes faithfulness and prohibits fruitfulness. Fear originates deep in the pits of hell. Evil would have us change our focus from the promised abundance of God to the pathetic amount of goods that we hold tightly in our hands. The rich young man chose to cling tightly to what he held in his hand instead of letting go to the abundant purpose and promise of God. He believed in Jesus but chose not to follow Jesus. Many of our people will make the same decision. Do not let this discourage **Fear paralyzes faithfulness and prohibits fruitfulness. Fear originates deep in the pits of hell.** you or cause you to stop short of challenging people to follow Jesus in whole-hearted obedient devotion!

Devotion is a matter of priority. We will never discover financial freedom until we seek first the Kingdom of God. Jesus makes the incredible promise that if we serve God first, money will serve us. God will meet *all* of our needs (Matthew 6:33)! Having the courage to give is a true demonstration of faith and the expression of devotion. *"Where your treasure is, there your heart will be also"* (Matthew 6:21). If we wish to be complete, downsize, release to the hand of God, and give to the poor. We have power with God by our actions toward people. Jesus encouraged his followers, *"Whatever you did for one of the least of these brothers and sisters of mine, you did for me"* (Matthew 25:40).

Here is Economics 101, *"If you help the poor, you are lending to the Lord and he will repay you"* (Proverbs 19:17). God is not going to eternally bless people who are stingy, people who refuse to invest in God's interest of the poor, lost, and oppressed. God's promise is for the generous. *"A generous person will prosper; whoever refreshes others will be refreshed"* (Proverbs 11:25).

Have you ever wondered why God commands his people to, *"Bring the full tithe into the storehouse"* (Malachi 3:10)? The answer comes next, *"that there may be food in my house."* This is really an issue of biblical economics as it relates to meeting the needs of the orphan and widow. When God's people are faithful in bringing the full tithe (10

percent) into the church, the church can faithfully carry out its mission in proclaiming the good news to the poor and bringing release to the captives. This is truly the nature and purpose of Christ's Church, based on the people of Jesus having the right focus of devotion. *"All the believers were one in heart and mind. No one claimed that any of their possessions was their own, but they shared everything they had"* (Acts 4:32). This demonstration of heart devotion was the reason the early church operated with such miraculous power and why new converts were added on a daily basis.

When we put God first, money will serve us. If not, we will always remain enslaved to money and debt. Financial freedom begins in the heart. Our people will never know financial freedom until they realize that financial freedom is a matter of heart devotion. Seek God first. Serve God first. When we put God first, money will serve us. If not, we will always remain enslaved to money and debt.

The Commitment to Debt-free Living

Debt is one of the greatest forces of oppression. This oppression prohibits a majority of the people we minister to from living in the freedom and abundance of generous discipleship. One of the critical disciplines that must be practiced in order to live debt-free is the ability to articulate and focus on commitments that live beyond immediate gratification. The long-range commitment to help your children  attain a college education, for instance, is a worthy goal that makes current sacrifice worth the pain and effort.

Any debt that you acquire, however, mortgages your future. You either pay now or you pay later. Later always comes at a much higher price! Debt is always about immediate gratification. When Jesus was in his time of wilderness testing, the tempter appealed to his immediate appetites and passions: *Jesus, you don't need the cross. You can have the world and everything in it without going through all this prolonged nonsense of discipline, pain, and delayed gratification.* That is why it is so easy to reach for the plastic credit card. We are tempted to believe that we can have what we do not have the current means to afford; to experience the benefits of immediate gratification without the payment. "What's the cost? We'll talk about that later. Have it now and we'll settle later." *Later* always demands that we pay homage to the devil. Debt is slavery! *"The rich rule the poor, and the borrower is a servant to the lender"* (Proverbs 22:7).

I was returning from an out-of-town speaking engagement and called my wife from the airport to tell her when to expect me home. I had been looking forward to a quiet Friday evening at home with the opportunity for the first seasonal fire in the fireplace on a crisp fall evening. "Well, the furnace guys are here," she said with a tone of utter frustration. "We need to buy a new furnace. The one we have is past repair."

I could hardly believe my ears! Just two weeks prior, the sump pump in our basement had gone out, resulting in a flood that required us to purchase all new carpet. Like the bumper sticker says, "Dung Happens" (loose translation).

We read of a woman in 2 Kings 4 who was not prepared for the unexpected. She and her husband were settled into the day-to-day routine of "living the dream," raising sons, paying the bills, and accumulating debt, when the unexpected happened. This woman was in no way prepared to deal with the ensuing crisis of her husband's death. In the ancient culture a woman without a husband had no means of support. And her children would be sold into slavery for any debts that the husband had accumulated. Poverty was a certainty for widows unless the community intervened (by leaving a tithe of crops for the widows and orphans), or unless someone showed her how to take initiative, as the prophet did here. In our present-day culture this could be the story of a family who works hard to stay afloat in the immediate without creating a plan for future contingencies, even loss of an income provider. Like many of the people in our churches, families today do not live at their means but beyond their means. Common sense tells us that we can't spend more than we make but the tempter appeals to our appetites and passions. Debt has nothing to do with common sense.

Common sense tells us that we can't spend more than we make but the tempter appeals to our appetites and passions. Debt has nothing to do with common sense.

Here is the key to financial freedom: you cannot live *at* your means. When you live at your means, you are spending everything that comes in and have absolutely no recourse when the unexpected happens. You then must spend what you don't have, to replace the flood-soaked carpet and the unrepairable furnace. The commitment to live debt-free requires a strategic commitment to live *below* your means. The widow explains what happens when you don't. *My husband has died, I am out of money, and I can't pay all this debt. We were a two-income family and now the creditors are coming after my two sons* (2 Kings 4:1). Church leaders must help their congregations understand that when we mortgage our own futures, we jeopardize our children's futures.

Keep a future focus! Remember that our responsibility is to position our children for God's picture of life-long success. As parents, if we are not purposefully holding to a disciplined lifestyle motivated by a future focus, our twenty-one-year-old children will set out into their own cycle of financial slavery!

When we live below our means we are able to position all of God's children for a better future.

As church leaders we must lift up God's faithfulness by telling the stories of persons who are living *below* their means. For example, Jim owns a Ford dealership and is very committed to Jesus' mission of feeding the poor and setting the oppressed free. He traveled with me to investigate our 3000-acre agricultural project in the Darfurian region of the Sudan. "If you do the math, our $327,000 investment will provide for over 26,000 people this year," he pointed out. "That means $1,200 will buy a year of life for 100 children!" As Jim astutely pointed out, when we live below our means we are able to position all of God's children for a better future.

Evil's sole objective is to lure you to go for the instant impulse, because Evil's purpose is to steal, kill, and destroy. The issue of God's people living debt-free is a very literal life or death issue for the children living in the displacement camps in the Sudan. Debt-free living is not just about positioning our own biological children for success, but *all* of God's children! We exist as disciples of Jesus to be channels of God's blessings in the world. The apostle Paul reminds us, *"Let no debt remain outstanding, except the continuing debt to love one another, for whoever loves others has fulfilled the law"* (Romans 13:8). In the true biblical sense, loving other people is not, "Oh, I feel good about you and have warm fuzzy feelings."

You can't be a life-giver if you are an enslaved borrower. Love is manifest in acts of sacrifice to meet the specific needs of hurting people. You cannot deploy acts of sacrifice to meet the needs of others if you are living at or beyond your means. You can't be a life-giver if you are an enslaved borrower.

Elisha describes a strategic stewardship plan to help the widow begin her path to financial freedom. He begins by asking her a question that becomes the catalyst for the first step in debt-free living. *"What do you have in your house"* (v.2)? Remember that the widow in the ancient world was the deceased husband's property and seldom had any way of earning money. Bring her, however, into current times, and the widow's response probably goes something like this: *Well, that's the whole issue. I don't make enough money. My husband died, and if I just had some way to make more money I wouldn't be in this mess.*

Getting out of debt isn't about making more money, it's about spending less than you make. It's difficult to control how much money you make, but you can control how much you spend. The Spirit will bring into our lives the lesson of contentment. *"I have learned to be content whatever the circumstances. I know what it is to be in need, and I know what it is to*

Until our people learn Contentment 101 God is not going to promote them to Blessings 202.

have plenty. I have learned the secret of being content in any and every situation, whether well-fed or hungry, whether living in plenty or want. I can do all this through him who gives me strength" (Phil. 4:11-13). Until our people learn Contentment 101 God is not going to promote them to Blessings 202.

Abundance is an inside-out proposition, not outside-in. God wants us to develop attitudes of gratitude, learning to trust God with what we already have "in our house." Our people must seek the accountability and encouragement found in the support of the faith community. Elisha challenges the woman to enlist the support of her neighbors, *"Go around and ask all your neighbors for empty jars. Don't ask for just a few"* (v. 3). Many of our people will fail totally in their endeavor to break the addictive cycle of debt if they do not have the support of community. I am often surprised by the number of people in my congregation who tell me that they don't know how to make a budget. It is probably a similar statistic in your church. From Elisha we perceive a clue about how to help. Elisha was strategically connecting the woman to people in the community, who could help her measure out the little bit that she had to left for food. In our congregation we do this through cell groups, free financial counseling, and Crown Financial Ministries classes. Learning to be faithful with the little that God has entrusted to us will provide the means for the miraculous! Consider how this is working for one couple in our church family, Kathi and Randy.

> (Kathi) *Randy and I met and fell in love and we decided to get married. We had both been previously married.*
>
> (Randy) *Together we both brought a lot of debt into the relationship.*
>
> (Kathi) *We thought love would erase all that. We don't need to worry about that. We have four children, we sent them to college, and so I had parent loans.*
>
> (Randy) *We had some investment properties, and we had student loans.*
>
> (Kathi) *The oldest went to graduate school, so we helped there.*
>
> (Randy) *We had credit card debt. When we first came together, we probably had close to $480,000 worth of total debt.*

(Kathi) We just brought it all to the table to add it up, and I tell you I think I hyperventilated.

(Randy) Kathi had passed out on the floor. I had to pick her up, and then it was, like, how do you get in this kind of financial position? And so, the first place we turned to was the church.

(Mike Slaughter) There is no greater indicator of your true values and priorities than what you do with your money.

(Kathi) And we were thinking, this is what we need.

(Randy) That's where we started getting resolution about our situation. Mike told us we need to deal with our debt right now. We started with a "Get Out of Debt" class, and then we ended up being in a Crown Class. During the Crown Class, we learned that it's not our money to begin with, and God asks us to trust everything to God's care. The only thing that God asks is that we give God 10 percent.

(Kathi) We started at 10 percent from the top, from that week on.

(Randy) We quit going out, eating out as much. We started saving all of our change.

(Kathi) We absolutely quit using credit cards.

(Randi) We average probably about $500 a year in change.

(Kathi) We started doing coupons; we planned meals.

(Randy) Do we need all the television channels we have?

(Kathi) We have a lot of magazine subscriptions, and we wondered why do we have all of that? We know how much comes into the house and how much goes out, to the penny. He's a receipt freak. We have envelopes and a budget. There's an envelope for the car and there's one for gardening. The area that we're looking at this time is our cable bill.

(Randy) We have gone from one extreme to another, and now we're at this point where we really have the hope of being out of debt. The next plan will be, What do we do with our time and money and resources for God that we don't have to give to the past.

(Kathi) We have been so blessed by being obedient.

(Randy) You see the light at the end of the tunnel, the hope. We feel good that we're on that right track.[1]

Giving people hope is the mission of the Church! A couple that was almost a half million dollars in debt has reduced that debt by 60 percent in three years. Many others are finding the same freedom in their money matters through the stewardship program that is outlined in this resource.

[1] View Randy's and Kathi's story on the companion DVD in this book.

In 2 Kings 4, Elisha continues to direct the widow's efforts through a strategic plan for debt-free living. How did God provide for this woman's great need? Did he wave a magic wand? Ensure a winning lottery ticket?

Our contribution of work is the means through which God provides for our daily needs and builds our self-esteem.

Would the widow awaken to find the money under the Christmas tree? Sadly, there is no magical pain-free solution to getting out of debt. Elisha encouraged the widow to find a job, to use her God-given creativity to generate an industry.

As part of changing the attitudes of our heart, some of our people must change their perspective about work. You will never be a star performer if you view work as an unpleasant necessity that must be tolerated and plodded through until weekend relief arrives. Our contribution of work is the means through which God provides for our daily needs and builds our self-esteem. Our daily work is to be an act of worship. We serve God and have the opportunity to bless people through the efforts of our labors. The word *liturgy* (worship), means "people-work." How did God provide the increase in the woman's life? *"They brought the jars to her and she kept pouring"* (v. 5). The widow kept working! Work is God's means for supplying your miracle in your congregation.

Whatever you do, work at it with all your heart, as working for the Lord, not for human masters...

Colossians 3:23

KEEP pouring

Maximize the opportunity! *"'When all the jars were full,' she said to her son, 'bring me another one.' But he replied, 'There is not a jar left.' Then the oil stopped flowing"* (vs. 6). I often wonder what would have happened if the woman would have collected more jars. God's picture is always bigger than ours. The Bible challenges us to do all things with excellence, to continually pursue God's best. Debt-free living is a commitment to keep pouring, to persevere through the temptations of immediate gratification towards the promise of Christ's abundant future.

Debt-free living is a commitment to keep pouring, to persevere through the temptations of immediate gratification towards the promise of Christ's abundant future.

The Practice of Discipline

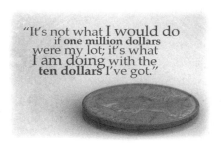

Financial freedom is not about how much or how little we have. Fiscal freedom is the consequence of being faithful and disciplined with what God has given us. As my grandfather would say, "It's not what I'd do if $1,000,000 were my lot; it's what I'm doing with the $10 that I've got!"

"It's not what I would do if one million dollars were my lot; it's what I am doing with the ten dollars I've got."

We are entrusted with God's resources and will be held accountable for producing a return on God's investment. *"Again, it will be like a man going on a journey who called his servants and entrusted his wealth to them. To one he gave five bags of gold, to another two bags, and to another one bag, each according to his ability"* (Matthew 25:14-15). The issue of money and possessions is really an issue of ownership. For whom do we work? To whom am I responsible? Did you notice the part in Jesus' parable, *"entrusted his wealth to them"*? We are entrusted with God's resources and will be held accountable for producing a return on God's investment. Notice the master's response to the servant that threw God's resources down a hole; *"You wicked, lazy servant! So you knew that I harvest where I have not sown and gather where I have not scattered seed? Well then, you should have put my money on deposit with the bankers, so that when I returned I would have received it back with interest"* (v. 26-27).

God feeds hungry people, reaches the lost, and sets oppressed people free through the resources (seed) that we release from our hands. I've heard Christian people pray for starving children around the world, and then wonder why God is not doing more to stop famine and genocide. God entrusts resources into our hands so that we invest them to

I harvest where I have not sown and gather where I have not scattered seed...

Matthew 25:26

meet the needs of the world. That is what Jesus meant when he said, *"I harvest where I have not sown and gathered where I have not sown seed"* (Matthew 25:26). God depends on the faithful sowing of the seed that God has placed in our hands!

Every good farmer knows that you can't eat all of your seed. You must set aside working seed to sow to future harvest. Let's say for the sake of easy math, you made $100 this week. The first 10 percent (tithe) goes to the

Lord as the demonstration of devotion. *"Bring the whole tithe...that there may be food in my house."* Remember why God needs food in his house? How else

God entrusts resources into our hands so that we invest them to meet the needs of the world.

can God feed the hungry childen in the Sudan? How else can God take the good news of the gospel to people who have never heard?

Now the second 10 percent should be set aside as working seed, seed that will be sown for a future harvest. The first of the baby boomers (born in 1946) turned age 60 in 2006. This post World War II generation that has defined much of current culture is facing a retirement that they have not provided for and experiencing benefit cutbacks that they have not

planned on. *"The man who had received five bags of gold went at once and put his money to work and gained five bags more. So also, the one with two bags of gold gained two more"* (v.16-17). Fruitfulness is the result of disciplined faithfulness!

Now we come to the test of true discipline, setting the standard of our lifestyles below the 80 percent of our remaining income. (Remember that you must allow for the unexpected.) People must be given practical action steps for outlining a strategic disciplined financial plan. Here are the action steps that I name from the pulpit each year:

1. **Do the right first thing: planned giving to God.** At the beginning of each year, determine that the first line item of your budget will be the amount you are going to give on a weekly basis. Write that amount down and stick to your plan. *"On the first day of every week each one of you should set aside a sum of money in keeping with your income"* (1 Corinthians 16:2). Never offer God the leftovers; take the first right action!

2. **Seek a wise mentor or an accountability group.** I've done this in any area of my life that required serious change. When I was forty-nine my body fat was 38 percent. I don't know how many times through the years I tried to change my lifestyle habits without knowing how to proceed or sustain the effort. I needed a trainer, someone who was accomplished in the area that I wasn't. This time I connected with a personal trainer, and five years later at age fifty-four my body fat was between 14-15 percent. Seek a mentor, and provide mentors in financial accountability for your congregation! You can enable this strategy by offering "Get Out of Debt" classes.

3. **Write a budget.** The first step in developing a budget is to list all debt. Go through all set expenses and determine what you can do without. Do you really need all of those newspaper and magazine subscriptions? How many of us could take a smaller selection package on cable TV? Can you eat out less often? How about eliminating your land phone line and using only your cell phone? Can you do without lawn service? Take an honest look at what you can do without. Don't forget to budget for entertainment, vacations, and gift-buying for the year.

4. **Perform plastic surgery.** Cut up your credit cards and assume no new debt. We do not honor God, other people, or our own children's future when we continue to live beyond our means.

5. **Set future goals.** Give examples from your own life about this habit. For example, in *Money Matters: Financial Freedom for All God's Children*, I describe my purchase of a new Harley Davidson Motorcycle with cash. It was the culmination of a ten-year dream for which I saved; the fruit of delayed gratification. It felt good to pay cash, not risking my children's future education, and enabling our family to continue to give sacrificially to Christ's mission of reaching the lost and setting oppressed people free.

6. **Nurture an attitude of gratitude.** List everything you already have for which you are thankful. The idols of greed and materialism will always tempt you to desire what belongs to another.

7. **Pray! Pray! Pray!** Those who prove faithful with a few things will be trusted with much! Here is the story of a young couple who are demonstrating the freedom that comes from the practice of discipline, Lance and Amber.

> *(Lance) Amber and I met in college and got married, and right away we started having to live off credit cards. Debt just started to build. We didn't have any sense of a budget. We had no idea of where our money was going. And so by the time we graduated from college, the debt was just getting bigger and bigger. The more we would try to say, "Well, we're just going to spend less," nothing would happen because we didn't have a plan.*
>
> *After three years of law school we moved to the Dayton area. Just our credit card debt, not our student loans, was at $20,000. The only thing that we had to show for it by the time we got to Ohio was a washer, dryer, and our bed. That was it!*

Everything else was just gone. In college we spent it on eating, going to the movies, or buying gifts for people at Christmas when we should have said, "No, we don't have the money, and that's not what it is about." We were working to pay off stuff we didn't even have any more.

Once we got to our church we signed up for the stewardship campaign. But then we faced a dilemma, which was, "How much do we give?" versus "How much do we use to get out of debt?" We prayed about it, and talked about it and finally came to the conclusion that we're going to give as if we don't have the debt, and we will work out our debt reduction around our giving. So we started giving 10 percent. We thought that was what we should do.

We sat down and had a serious budget meeting. We met in the office for three hours and just hashed it out. "Okay, how are we going to do this?" For each month we can set aside "X" amount of dollars for this and "X" amount of dollars for that. For eating out, it was $30 a month. We'd go out to eat once. We loved, after church, going out to eat with friends. Once a month we can do that. The other three or four weeks, sorry we have to go home. Our food budget is out. And so we'd have to go home. For us personally, whether it was to get some clothes or whatever, it was ten bucks a month. If you wanted something that was $50, you were going to have to wait five months. It was brutally hard. That's just how it had to be.

The numbers don't add up. There's no other explanation for us, other than it was God taking care of us because we were now walking in the road that he wanted us to walk. We had the resources to get out of debt, and we didn't go without what we needed.

Neither one of us got any raises. Amber works as a teacher and I work for the county. As lawyers go I don't make a third of what I could make at a private firm if I had gone that route. But somehow those loaves and fishes multiplied to where the debt is dead and we gave more than we thought we ever could have given.

Amber's car is now paid for. It's phenomenal. It's an extra bunch of money each month that we didn't have yesterday. Amber and I have been married about nine and a half years. We're now expecting our first child in a couple of months. When the baby comes, we're not going to still be spending most of our money each month to pay for movies we went to in college. We can use that money to provide for our child. And instead of looking backwards all the time each month, our finances and our lives can be looking forward to whatever the Lord has in store for us.[2]

Jesus was always focused on liberating individuals from paralyzing addictions and binding oppressions. Jesus ministers to people in the places where they are hurting. Jesus was always focused on liberating individuals from paralyzing addictions and binding oppressions. Conversely, materialism creates an oppressive burden of debt that hinders God's people from generous fruitful living. Remember, oh trusted Shepherd of God's People, your job is not to raise money for a church budget. Yours is the unique privilege of setting the oppressed free. Jesus is in the business of giving hope—one life at a time!

[2] View Lance and Amber's story on the companion DVD in this book.

Chapter Three

Implementing a Year-round Strategic Stewardship Program

There are a number of vital priorities I heartily espoused when I accepted the call into ordained ministry. Implementing a comprehensive stewardship program, however, was not one of them. I definitely wanted to make disciples. I deeply desired to follow Jesus into the heroic mission of winning the lost and setting oppressed people free. I simply had no idea that money would really matter as I set out to pastor one of God's churches.

Despite my early naiveté, however, I have now come to realize that people's attitudes about money and possessions are at the root of any discipleship issue. I am now able to see that only as I address all issues of life, including how money is handled, can I be truly used by God to set oppressed people free. It is as I've discovered the enslaving affects of materialism that I've become passionate and bold about money matters. To be effective in Christ's mission, pastors and church leaders must talk about money, and we need a strategic approach to training people in the area of responsible money management.

In this chapter I will share with you the systematic annual stewardship program developed over the years at Ginghamsburg Church. This strategic, intentional yearly plan has proven effective in liberating our people from the bondage of debt while simultaneously increasing the outreach of

Only as I address all issues of life, including how money is handled, can I be truly used by God to set oppressed people free.

our church's mission in exponential ways. In my tenure at Ginghamsburg Church our annual budget has increased from $27,000 to approximately $5,000,000 annually. A budget of this size represents an incredible opportunity to meet the real needs of people in Jesus' power and love!

The annual stewardship plan can be implemented in small churches too, which is one reason why the publisher offers the entire program at a low expense, self-contained in two books, with customizable resources provided on the DVD that is included in this book.

Stewardship Begins with Me!

We each have the propensity to rationalize about money. For example, Carolyn and I were married after my junior year of college. I was working part time as a youth minister in my home church, and she was working as a home economist at a local company near my university. We began marriage with the commitment to assume no credit card debt that could not be paid in full at the end of each month. We also made the commitment to save something out of each paycheck, no matter how small. From the first day of our marriage we adhered to a rigorous budget that included quarterly tuition payments, insurance, rent, utilities, and miscellaneous expenses. We were careful in including everything we could think of in our budget, including allowances for gifts and vacations. However, we did not prioritize tithing as the first fiscal commitment. I don't really remember what we gave that first year or what percentage of our income it represented.

> **How could we possibly afford to tithe? "God would understand," I rationalized to myself.**

During the second year of our marriage we headed off to seminary. We continued to drive back to our home church on weekends, where I still served as the youth minister. Carolyn had to take a job in the local seminary community for less than half the pay of the previous year. My tuition tripled from what I had been paying to attend a local state university, and we were living on about half of what we had made the year before. How could we possibly afford to tithe? "God would understand," I rationalized to myself. "After all, the money that I am spending on a seminary education is for God."

> **"I want to ask you young women and men a question," he said as he methodically placed his glasses back on the bridge of his nose and peered over the top rim. "Are any of you cheating God?"**

I have great memories from my seminary years. Lifelong friendships were made, and an eternal calling was forged. I could hardly wait to get through that last semester and on to my first full-time appointment. One of the last elective courses that I took was a class in English Bible. Robert Traina was the professor, a brilliant man, who rarely deviated from his planned agenda. I do not know what possessed him to drift from his lecture plan on that May morning, a little more than a week from my graduation. As if speaking to me alone, he stepped away from his podium and removed his glasses. "I want to ask you young women and men a question," he said as he methodically placed his glasses back on the bridge of his nose and peered over the top rim. "Are any of you cheating God?" A silence permeated the air for what seemed to be an awkwardly indefinable amount of time. "If you are not giving God the full tithe, then you are cheating God. I ask that you have the integrity not to go into vocational ministry if you cannot obey God in such a simple matter."

I could not believe what I was hearing or how I could have been so foolish! Robert Traina's words resound in my spirit today. "If you cannot be faithful in the small things, then you cannot be trusted with greater things!" I found a place of solitude that very day and renewed my commitment to be a faithful steward of all that God had entrusted to me. I wrote in the back of my Bible, "Lord God, I promise from this day forward that I will always write the first check for the first 10 percent to you—Michael Slaughter, May 1976."

How about you? Are you being a faithful steward of what God has entrusted to you? Are you faithfully tithing, or are you cheating God? What is your current debt status? Have you made a commitment to live free from all credit card debt? Do you have a budget to which you are faithfully adhering? This might be a good time to set this book down, find a place of solitude, and renew your commitment to be a faithful steward of all that God has entrusted to you. Remember, you can't take anyone farther than you yourself have gone. A strategy for effective stewardship in your church begins with you!

Remember, you can't take anyone farther than you yourself have gone. A strategy for effective stewardship in your church begins with you!

Stewardship is Modeled Through Church Leadership

The selection of faithful, effective leaders is one of the most critical functions of ministry. Faithful leaders energize the mission of the local church as well as provide living models of the embodiment of Jesus' presence and purpose. I am a Christian today because of the sacrifice of the faithful servants of Christ whom I experienced in the church. In the same way, unfaithful leaders can sabotage the church's mission and render the gospel message impotent.

The pastor must make leadership selection and development one of the first priorities of her or his strategic plan. In the United Methodist system the pastor is the chair of the annual nominations committee. In other traditions the same

It is absolutely essential that we place no one in a leadership position who is not both filled with God's Spirit and faithful in stewardship.

role applies. It is absolutely essential that we place no one in a leadership position who is not both filled with God's Spirit and faithful in stewardship. I have made it a point, from my first day in ministry, to know what people give. When I first came to my congregation, I found the godfathers and godmothers who sat on the board threatening to quit giving if I continued to press for change. But they were giving next to nothing. Guess what? They did quit giving, but at the end of the year the total offerings of the church increased. I have seen this happen again and again when churches quit operating out of fear and begin to appoint leaders and leadership boards based on sound biblical faithfulness.

I can hear a few pastors grumbling about whether the pastor should know what persons give, and the controversy that this may stir up with some of the people, but I encourage you to look at it in a different light. When I go to the doctor for a complete physical, the nature of the exam is very personal. I don't believe that I need to be more explicit. The doctor cannot make an accurate diagnosis if he or she doesn't have all of the information. My physical well being is dependent upon my doctor having

As ministers of the gospel, we are spiritual doctors. very personal, complete, and confidential information. My life depends upon it! As ministers of the gospel, we are spiritual doctors. We cannot give proper guidance to a person's spiritual well-being without having the right personal information.

Jesus was very aware of a person's giving practices. *"As Jesus looked up, he saw the rich putting their gifts into the Temple treasury. He also saw a poor widow put in two very small copper coins. 'Truly I tell you,' he said, 'this poor widow has put in more than all the others. All these people gave their gifts out of their wealth; but she out of her poverty put in all she had to live on.'"* (Luke 21:1-4).

Giving is a spiritual issue. Money matters are a priority of the heart. My job as pastor is to make sure that all those who are in the important position of decision-making and direction-giving are faithfully tithing. Tithing is a true demonstration of personal priorities and reveals any potential leader's buy-in to the values and direction of the local church. Tithing reveals their ultimate ability to be faithful in the courageous execution of the mission of Jesus. Many times we have identified very capable persons whom we

Many times we have identified very capable persons whom we thought would be great additions to our leadership team but changed our mind after we checked their giving records.

thought would be great additions to our leadership team but changed our mind after we checked their giving records. Remember what Jesus said, *"For where your treasure is, there your heart will be also"* (Matthew 6:21). Sometimes all the person needs is more time to grow spiritually. We have come back to some of these persons a few years later and found that they had grown in the area of faithful stewardship and were now ready to lead the church in a strategic position on our leadership board. Be careful that you do not promote these persons too quickly, lest the whole ministry suffer!

We apply this standard of tithing as the expectation for all of the leaders of the church, although there are many areas where people can serve before they grow to this level in their faith journey. It is important to distinguish between a worker position and a leadership position of greater influence and responsibility. From classroom teachers to cell group leaders, the influence we transmit through our lifestyle practices is far greater than our words alone. Discipleship is caught much more than it is taught. Our practice is for every supervisor to sit down with the staff and unpaid servant leaders on their teams and periodically review stewardship health. The leaders of your church are the key to growing a vital mission that is dependent on faithful steward-ship. These leaders become the models, advocates, and promoters of that same faithful stewardship. Seventy to eighty percent of your church resources will come from the leadership of your church.

It's time for a heart check-up. How are your board, elders, and/or staff acting in the area of stewardship? This is the area that may require your initial atten-tion as you lead your congregation forward in financial responsibility. It is a great place to start, using the material in this resource as a study guide. Remember that your church will never go beyond your leadership team. Consider who might currently be on your leadership team who is not willing to grow, thus needing to be tactfully removed. I pray for you to have the wisdom and courage to lead in these money matters!

> **Remember that your church will never go beyond your leadership team.**

Stewardship as an Expectation of Membership

It costs something to be a follower of Jesus Christ. *"If any want to become my follow-ers, let them deny themselves and take up their cross daily and follow me"* (Luke 14:26). Jesus was always calling people to calculate the cost of true discipleship. As I wrote in *Spiritual Entrepreneurs*, "Jesus was not a pop psychologist, hawking a gospel of individ-ualistic positive thinking. He was calling people to become part of a counter-culture in a covenant community. Membership would involve forsak-ing individual goals and agendas for the sake of a purpose, the Kingdom of God. When a church gets serious about renewal, it begins to ask new questions about the responsibilities of membership. Membership cannot and must not be separated from the cost of discipleship" (pg. 70-71).

> **When a church gets serious about renewal, it begins to ask new questions about the responsibilities of membership.**

After you examine your personal money matters and build a faithful steward-ship leadership team (board-elders-staff) it is time to focus on a systematic stewardship program for the entire church. A systematic strategy is a repeat-able strategy; it includes curriculum and can be taught by others. We developed a 13-week basic discipleship curriculum for people interested in pursuing the commitment of membership, called "A Follower's Life." Less than one-third of our weekly worship attendees have made a commitment to covenant community (membership). It costs something to be a follower of Jesus, and we don't apologize that it costs something to be a member of Jesus' body. The issue of stewardship and tithing is one of the issues that are dealt with during this three-month class. Other members of the church are invited into the class to share their own experience in tithing and give the participants an opportunity to ask questions. By including tithing in the pre-membership training, the expectation is set right up front.

Each person seeking to become a member of the church at the end of the 13-week session goes through an interview process. They are asked about four areas of their spiritual walk: their participation in worship, their connection to a cell group for encouragement and accountability, their place of service, and their commitment to tithe. If they are not currently tithing because of excessive debt, unemployment, or other issues, they are asked to provide a plan and timeline to get there. Remember that our goal is the ultimate health and liberation of people, not to use people for the sake of the institution. Developing trust is essential.

The Annual Stewardship Message Series

As I already mentioned in the opening chapter of this book, our attendance grows during our annual stewardship series. The attendance during the four weeks that I teach on Money Matters every November is surpassed in attendance only on Christmas and Easter weekends. We plan the annual series as a worship team, featuring strategic people in the church who are experiencing the liberating power of God in their financial lives. People long to hear and relate to stories of hope from people of varying backgrounds and social situations. We present these human stories in media form (See the list of "Stories of Faith and Freedom" that can be viewed on the DVD that comes with this book.)

We design an attractive direct-mail postcard (see Appendix, item 6; the source file can be copied from the DVD) for people who live in our targeted geographic area; a piece that hooks into their current life experience. We purchase a mailing list from a direct-mail company and specify households of persons aged 25 to 45, with children living in the home (This is our previously identified target audience for general ministry; your congregation's target may be different, but you need a target.). We also specify the zip codes to which we want to reach out strategically.

Once we've invited people to come and experience relevant biblical principles on financial freedom, we must build great worship experiences around this theme. We work hard to address the felt need of the people while staying true to the gospel message. We are empowering people to grow beyond materialistic consumption to esteem-building contribution.

The fourth weekend of every series always culminates with the opportunity for commitment, simultaneous to a time of Thanksgiving. Following the message and clear instructions, we allow for a time of quiet reflection, prayer-full moments for filling out the commitment card (see sample commitment card in the Appendix). On commitment weekend the offering is always taken at the end of the worship celebration so that people can place their commitment cards in the basket and those who do not make a commitment will not be made to feel awkward. I always point out that this commitment is for the Ginghamsburg family and those who feel connected to it; our visitors are not to feel obligated. Note that we invited visitors to observe examples of how Christian disciples have been liberated to make a difference. (See Chapter 4 for examples of worship themes and message outlines.)

> **We are empowering people to grow beyond materialistic consumption to esteem-building contribution.**

Get Out of Debt for Good Class

It is not enough to teach people about financial freedom and the joy that comes from sacrificial giving. We must also aggressively help them to deal with the oppressive burden of debt, under which they live. People struggle with giving not because they don't want to give but because they honestly don't know how to meet current financial obligations. "We began to get into trouble when I quit my job to have our two children," a young mother shared with me. "We used the credit card to pay for groceries and gasoline, and now we don't have anything to show for it!" Many persons in our churches still owe money for food that was eaten years before. They continue to pay interest to maintain the "privilege" of carrying the full balance of the principle. They persist in a vicious downward spiral, a lifestyle of hopeless slavery.

As part of our annual stewardship curriculum we have developed a three-week (one-hour session) class called Get Out Of Debt for Good. This class, as well as classes that use Crown Financial curriculum for small groups, has been a tremendous help to many of the persons

> **People struggle with giving not because they don't want to give but because they honestly don't know how to meet current financial obligations.**

seeking growth in our faith community. Randy and Kathi (see Chapter 2) were one such couple. You can obtain more information about starting Crown Financial Ministries in your church from this web site: http://www.crown.org/financialwisdom/church/startcrown.asp

Class Outlines: Get Out of Debt for Good

Week 1: What the Bible Says About Debt

A. Debt facts:

Simple review about the average percentages with Americans and credit card debt, savings, education and retirement preparation, etc.

B. What the Bible does not say about debt:

1. It is a sin to borrow.
2. It is wise to borrow.
3. God will bail you out of debt.
4. Debt is an exercise in faith.
5. It is a sin to loan money.

C. What the Bible does say about debt:

1. All borrowing must be repaid (Psalm 37:21).
2. Surety (guaranteeing or cosigning someone else's loan) is foolish (Proverbs 6:1-5; 11:15).
3. Debt always presumes upon the future and makes uncertain assumptions (James 4:13-15).

D. Some presumptions when borrowing:

1. My health will remain good.
2. My job will continue to provide income.
3. The asset borrowed against will continue to grow in value (margin debt).
4. The business I own will continue to generate a profit.
5. Borrowing may deny God an opportunity
   a. to expand your faith by trusting God's promise of provision or
   b. to allow you to experience the joy of God supplying others' needs through you.

Week 2: Types of Debt and Debt-making Decisions

A. Types of debt:

1. Credit card debt: High rates of interest (12-24 percent). Many companies will entice you with low beginning rates for a minimal period of time. Typically, no collateral required other than the credit worthiness of the borrower. Generally not tax deductible.

2. Installment debt: Generally used to buy higher-cost items such as furniture, cars, boats, with the item purchased being the collateral. Interest rates are generally lower than for credit cards, but still in the 8-15 percent range. The lender may repossess whatever is financed, should repayment fall behind. Repayment can extend upwards to 72 months (six years). Promotion stresses "easy repayment terms." Generally not tax deductible. What about 90 days same-as-cash or no interest for one year? If you have the cash in hand and can invest it for one year in a CD (certificate of deposit), it is a wise use of credit. Do not presume that you will have the money, however. This can result in the highest percentage of debt at the end of the grace period if you cannot make payment in full.

3. Mortgage debt: Typically used to buy a home. Rates vary from time to time and in recent years have stayed in the 4-8 percent range. Repayments may vary from 10 to 30 years and may be repaid biweekly or monthly. The house is the collateral. Generally tax deductible.
   a. Fixed rate mortgages: the interest rate does not change during the life of the loan.
   b. Adjusted rate mortgages: the interest rate changes periodically, generally on an annual basis. Most ARMs have a ceiling, or limit, as to how high the rate can go over the life of the loan. For example, you may have a 4 percent ARM, which can increase a maximum of 2 percent per year, with a maximum interest rate of 12 percent. Second mortgages/home equity loans generally have the same tax advantages as mortgage debt.

4. Investment debt: Used to buy something with which you hope to make a profit. The rate is usually between mortgage and credit card debt. Repayment is almost always fixed over a short period of time and may require fairly large payments compared to other forms of borrowing. Collateral may be a personal signature against other assets or the investment itself. Generally tax deductible, within limits.

5. Business debt: A business may borrow to buy furniture, fixtures, and equipment to expand facilities or to buy a building out of which to operate. It may also borrow to increase business in general (a working capital loan). Interest rates vary with the credit worthiness

of the borrower, and the terms of repayment depend on the negoti-
ations between borrower and lender. The assets of the business and
the personal guarantees of the owners for smaller companies usually
secure this type of debt. Generally tax deductible within the business
tax return.

6. Leases: Leasing can be viewed very similarly to installment debt, but at
   the end of the agreement you have no asset. Leasing can be strategic
   in the business setting. With the pace of change in technology your
   business might need to update equipment every year or two, which
   makes leasing a very viable option. But from a personal standpoint,
   computers can be used for a very long time.

7. Rent to own: More costly than installment debt. This is an industry that
   takes advantage of the poor and those with weak credit histories. You
   end up paying two to three times more for a product than you would
   if you had cash in hand.

B. Decision-Making Rules:
   The reason we consider going into debt is to meet a need or desire that
   has become a high priority for us. Sometimes, the temptation to use credit
   to meet the perceived need overwhelms both common sense and spiritual
   convictions. Weighing today's desires against future benefits is a classic
   definition of maturity.

1. The rule of common sense: When it comes to credit card debt and
   installment debt, the economic return is never greater than the cost
   of borrowing. The interest rate is too high, and the items purchased
   or consumed only depreciate in value. In other words, you will end up
   continuing to pay for purchases in the future that have already been
   consumed or have no value! Mortgage debt on the other hand is different. The home purchased should continue to increase in value. The
   consideration on investment debt needs to be made based on the
   earnings generated by the investment being greater than the cost of
   the loan. Borrow money at 12 percent on an investment guaranteed
   to earn 15 percent. Good idea? Look for a guaranteed investment!
   Same logic applies to a business loan. The items purchased with the
   loan should provide a return that is greater than the cost of the loan.
   Common sense 101: If it sounds too good to be true—it probably is!

2. A guaranteed way to repay: Remember the biblical principle that
   debt presumes upon the future. Financing our homes with a mortgage means the bank gets the house back if we can't pay. That is a
   guaranteed repayment plan! Using a credit card for convenience
   when you know that the money is in the bank to pay the full balance

after 30 days is a guaranteed way to repay. In all other situations you are taking an unnecessary risk by presuming the future.

3. Peace of heart and mind: Do you have peace in your heart and spirit? *"Let the peace of Christ rule in your hearts...and be thankful"* (Colossians 3:15). Listen to the still inner voice of the Spirit of God. Are you confused about making a purchase, uneasy about signing the contract? God is not the author of confusion. Nothing can make for a better lifestyle than peace of heart and mind!

4. Unity: A husband and wife should be in complete unity when it comes to purchasing and borrowing decisions.

Week 3: How to Get Out of Debt

A. Pray: At the risk of sounding too churchy, this is always the best first step, no matter what decisions we are looking to make. We need to seek the Lord's help, guidance, wisdom and discernment as we move to becoming debt free.

B. Establish a written budget: Budgets are not just for businesses. A written budget allows you to accurately connect real income with expenses and purchasing commitments. A written budget forces you to plan ahead, analyze your spending patterns and control the biggest cause of credit card debt—impulse buying! There are some great computer programs: Quicken, Microsoft Money, Excel. These can help in planning and budget tracking. There is also the unsophisticated envelope method that can work well. When you develop a budget, the tithe comes first. Use the 10/10/80 method. The first ten is given to the Lord and the second ten goes into savings for the future. Any farmer understands how he must not make the stupid mistake of consuming all of the seed from current income. Seed needs to be set aside as working seed for the purpose of sowing to future harvest. We then need to live off the remaining 80 percent. Remind people that they need to account for unexpected emergencies out of the 80 percent. Expenses paid annually or quarterly need to be accounted for and saved on a monthly basis. To figure vacations, gifts, insurance premiums or medical allowances divide by 12.

1. List all your assets, everything you own: The earth is the Lord's and everything in it. We are merely stewards of what God has entrusted us with. Evaluate your assets to determine if there is anything you do not need that might be sold to get you out of debt quickly. Garage sales and eBay are two quick sources. Boat, golf clubs, extra TVs, cars, etc. Just like Elijah asked the widow in 2 Kings 4 (see Chapter 2 of this book), "What do you have in your house?"

2. List all your liabilities, everything you owe: Many people are out of touch with their total amount of debt. It is really human nature to avoid unpleasant things. Many take the "ostrich" approach to their debt: stick their head into the sand and pretend the debt is not there. Listing your debts is a huge first step to establishing a repayment plan. You should list the creditor, amount of debt, due date, monthly payment, and interest rate.

3. Establish a debt repayment schedule for each creditor: Most debtors are willing to work with customers who are attempting to pay them back. While establishing this plan, ask for a renegotiation of the interest rate. There are two schools of thought when it comes to paying down debt: paying off the smallest debts first or paying off the higher interest rate

first. When a debt is paid off, the amount of its payment is applied to the next debt, and so on. The money freed up from repayment of a debt does not get put back into the general budget; it is applied to the next debt.

4. Consider earning extra income: For some people, extra hours at work or a second job might be the only short-term solution. If this becomes a necessity, decide in advance that all income earned will be used to pay off current debt. Make sure the new source of income does not harm your relationship with the Lord or with your family.

5. Accumulate no new debt: From this point forward, pay for everything with cash, check, or debit card at the time of purchase. Statistics show that people spend more when using credit cards, instead of cash. We call this phase of the plan "plastic surgery." Cut up all but one of your credit cards. Having one credit card for true emergencies is acceptable. Remember, do not get sucked into 90 days or one year same-as-cash offers.

C. Be content with what you have: 1 Timothy 6:6 says, *"Godliness with contentment is great gain."* We live in a culture where the advertising industry has devised powerful, sophisticated methods to entice the consumer to buy. Here are three trusted truisms:

1. The more TV you watch, the more you spend.
2. The more you look at catalogues and magazines, the more you spend.
3. The more you shop, the more you spend.

D. Consider a radical change in your lifestyle: What are you willing to give up in order to get out of debt? Lowering your standard of living significantly will allow you to get out of debt much more quickly. Could you live just as happily in a smaller home? Could you sell your new car with the high payment and drive an older car? Do you really need cable, cell phone, Internet access, and housecleaning or yard service? Do you need to go away for vacation? How about staying home and making day trips to the state park rather than the expensive amusement park. Can you use generic products just as easily as name brand products? Can you use coupons as a way to save money?

E. Do not give up: This may be the most difficult step of all. Getting out of debt is hard work. If it were easy, credit card companies would be going out of business. Remind the people that they have taken the important first initiative by coming to the class. Now encourage them to put their faith into action. At Ginghamsburg we encourage them to consider becoming part of a Crown Financial Ministries small group Bible study.

Annual Meetings with Key Investors

Twice a year I meet with the "Kingdom Investors" of my church for the purpose of accountability and vision casting. I have one set of meetings by invitation in the fall (See the sample letter, item 3 in the Appendix) with those who give $10,000 or more a year, and another set of soup and sandwich suppers with those who give $1,000 to $9,000 a year. These meetings are held each fall in conjunction with our annual stewardship series, for the purpose of communicating vision and gaining the ownership of these key givers.

It is important to keep it simple, because we want to assure our people that their trusted resources are going toward critical mission and not personal entertainment.

I usually meet with the top givers in someone's home or a nice room at the church, and we gather around simple refreshments and coffee. There are generally 20-40 people that attend in this more intimate setting. The number of givers that fall into the $1,000—9,000 category is obviously much larger, and we hold these meetings in a larger room (or worship area) at our church. Each of these simple soup and sandwich suppers (paper plates, plastic utensils with a donation basket at the end of the buffet table) generate a turn-out of 150 to 300 women and men. It is important to

Money follows mission, not budgets!

keep it simple, because we want to assure our people that their trusted resources are going toward critical mission and not personal entertainment. (It is also important to provide child care for the younger couples attending these meetings.) I believe these events are one of the most strategic initiatives for stewardship development and vision ownership in the local church. Eighty percent of your annual budget will come from this group of people.

Remember this important stewardship axiom: Money follows mission, not budgets! People are not interested in making sacrifices for tired church budgets, but they get very motivated by the opportunity to make a signifi-

With ever escalating utility costs, this will be a much more effective use of our stewardship resources, to multiply outward rather than expand inward.

cant impact in the lives of people for the sake of the mission of Jesus. This is why another one of my oft-repeated slogans at these investors meetings is "minimize brick and maximize mission." We carry out seven worship celebrations every weekend and are planning to expand that to sixteen within a year of this writing, by starting worship in café venues and house churches. With ever escalating utility costs, this will be a much more effective use of our stewardship resources, to multiply outward rather than expand inward. It energizes our investors when I remind them that we have to find creative alternatives, rather than embark into expensive building campaigns. This strategy provides maximum dollars for true mission. There are times, however, when you have no other alternative but to build (which is why I say "minimize brick" and not "eliminate brick"). Keep all building plans as simple and flexible as possible. Do not build any structure that could financially enslave future generations, thus tempting future leadership teams to serve the structure rather than the mission.

We bring both of these groups back together again in May for a picnic. This is a critical vision-casting opportunity that comes right before the summer slump in weekly offerings. I remind them at those **The pastor and leadership team cannot take stewardship development for granted!** picnics that ministry at our church steps up a notch in the summer with increased children's and student activities, camps and mission work projects. This is a great time to talk about vital children's and student ministries. Be as specific as possible in talking about impact: numbers reached and personal stories. The pastor and leadership team cannot take stewardship development for granted! The invitations for all Kingdom Investor meetings are sent with RSVP request (See sample invitations, items 3-6 in the Appendix). The names of those who haven't responded by a certain date are divided among the Leadership Board members to follow up with personal invitations by phone. We make it very clear that people are not going to be asked for money at these meetings. (See the sample phone script, item 8 in the Appendix.) Rather, because of their demonstrated commitment to the mission of Jesus through the church, they are being given the chance to hear about the direction of the church prior to the congregation as a whole. They will also be given the opportunity to give input and ask questions. I make this time with our loyal investors both informative and highly motivating. This is my opportunity as leader to show our investors the eternal, albeit measurable return on their Kingdom investment. Here is a sample meeting agenda outline for a fall Kingdom Investors meeting:

| Gathering: | 6:30 PM | —Table or living room conversation around dinner/ dessert |

Welcome: 7:00 PM   —Welcome the guests and give them a table discussion topic, which is stated something like this: "Take a moment to share with the people at your table some specific reason you choose to sacrificially invest in God's ministry through this church. (This is an excellent way for the spirit of the presentation to begin in a very positive upbeat manner. Faith grows as we hear others make positive professions!)

Presentation: 7:10 PM   —Use this as a time of reporting, inspiring, and vision casting. Remind the guests that they have been invited to this event because of their faithful demonstration of commitment to the mission of Jesus Christ expressed through your church. Share how as a leadership team we have the responsibility to give them a measurable, accountable reporting on their trusted investment. Make sure each person has received a copy of a comprehensive report prepared by yourself or your executive pastor (see sample Annual Report, item 6 in the Appendix). This excellent resource is more comprehensive and detailed than required during a conference with the district leader. It outlines real ministry accomplished, numbers of people reached, servants deployed, and so forth. They can read the reports when they get home, but being able to give them this printed piece demonstrates accountability and professionalism, deepening our relationship of trust.

As a leader, this is a great opportunity to inspire committed investors with stories of current success and vision for future direction. It is the leader's responsibility to articulate and cast the vision in the community of faith. Vision is born in leaders, not committees! The vision that God gives the leader precedes the setting of ministry goals and developing mission strategies and budgets. Alan Nelson in *Spirituality and Leadership* states, "A vision is a leader's mental image that conveys where an organization needs to be in the future. It primarily addresses the what, why, and when. 'How' follows. Vision is primarily right-brained and passionate. It evokes emotions. A result of vision is setting goals and developing strategy. It doesn't work the other way around."

"A vision is a leader's mental image that conveys where an organization needs to be in the future. It primarily addresses the what, why, and when. 'How' follows."

Now here is the part of vision that is critical to the success of your church's mission and stewardship initiative: "For a vision to be authentic, we can't feel fulfilled staying where we are for long. Four characteristics determine the quality of a vision: clarity, urgency, importance, and size. If any of these arenas is inadequate, you diminish the intensity of your vision and lessen the effect it has on your followers."[3]

Remind guests of your church's reason for existence, touching typically on such topics as: 1) the importance of equipping disciple-servant leaders, persons who are able to connect the presence and purpose of Jesus with the needs of others and empower future generations; 2) the true measure of our effectiveness as a church is not based on how many are attending, but by asking ourselves the question, "Are we reproducing disciple-servant leaders?"

At this point show two in-house video stories of mission that demonstrate your success during the past year in the missions area. Both stories would have been used as "mission moments" during your regular worship celebrations during that year. The leader's Kingdom Investor's presentation gives you a chance to highlight some of your most inspiring initiatives! Remember, people want to see in measurable ways that their sacrifice is making a difference. If you do not have the capability to do video presentations (someone in your congregation probably owns a camcorder and can put together a brief clip), you could do a live testimony at this point, but remember to rehearse it well, keeping it short and to the point. You don't want the inspiration to put people to sleep! This is why you try to use media whenever possible. (For ideas, you can view some sample stories of mission on the companion DVD in this book.)

Next, take the time to highlight your ministry's Key Focus for the coming year (for example "Maturity" or "Missions") and your need to focus on the inner

[3] (Navpress: Colorado Springs, 2002), p. 164.

journey of the heart in the coming year without neglecting the outward journey of mission. If the key focus is Maturity, for example, you might briefly point to the three areas of focus: 1) The spiritual disciplines of word, prayer, community, service, and stewardship; 2) the experience of community through cell group participation; 3) experimenting with two different expressions of church by starting new worship venues and house churches. Explain the importance of pioneering new expressions of church and worship that will be effective in reaching postmodern people in a post Christian world.

Save the best for last. Every church needs to commit itself to a heroic mission endeavor that will challenge its people to attempt the impossible and to give in faith.

Guests are given the opportunity to ask any questions or to give any input that they might have. I end the meeting in prayer promptly at 8:00 PM and stick around to talk to anyone that might have lingering questions. This format is very similar to the spring picnics mentioned above, with the exception of the written report.

The Monthly Stewardship Letter

Each month the Kingdom Investors (those who give $1000 a year or more) receive a letter that expresses appreciation for their continued sacrifice as well as updates on a current vital ministry endeavor. These letters never ask for money but encourage and show *specific* results of continued faithfulness. (See examples of monthly letters, items 11 and 12 in the Appendix).

Worship DVD Mission Moments

A three-minute video-clip, highlighting vital mission and ministry taking place through the church family is shown often during our worship celebrations. Most often it is shown before the offering. Money follows mission! (View video examples on the companion DVD included in this book).

Stewardship is a multilayered initiative that must be integrated in a holistic way into all dimensions of the congregation's life. There is not one stewardship program that fits all sizes. "Copy and paste" whatever may work from the program approach in this book, and then customize a stewardship program that is right for your setting.

Chapter Four

Sample Worship Celebrations and Message Outlines

Stewardship Worship Celebration 1: Devotion

Series: MONEY MATTER$

Word: Matthew 19

Felt Need: Fear and insecurity for my own life and well-being

Desired Outcome: To submit my life and heart to God as my first step in financial freedom

Theme: Devotion

Metaphor/Look: Series look—money clip with cross

Opening Music	Band/Gospel choir	Shabach[4]
Call to Worship/ Storytelling	Host *See scripts for sample.*	Matthew 19
Feature Worship Song	Band/Gospel choir	Total Praise[5]
Song Celebration	Band/Gospel choir	The Lord Reigns[6] I Choose to Praise You[7]
Updates/Video	Host	1) Get Out of Debt classes; 2) Mission Moment *Example: Sudan Miracle Minute video*
Offerings/Feature Song	Band/Gospel choir	Wonderful Is Your Name[8]
Video	On the Street	"What's Your Money Matter?"
Message	Pastor	Money Matter$:DEVOTION
Response/Send Out		The Lord Reigns
Exit Music	Band	TBD

---

[4] "Shabach," CCLI Song Number 1898392; Author Tobias Fox; © Copyright 1996 Lilly Mack Music.

[5] "Total Praise," Author Richard Smallwood, © Copyright T. Autumn Music/Zomba Songs Inc. (BMI).

[6] "The Lord Reigns," CCLI Song Number 119608; Authors Rick Founds and Todd Collins; © Copyright 1982 Maranatha! Music (Admin. by The Copyright Company).

[7] "I Choose to Praise You," Author Rita Baker, © Rita Baker @ www.ritabakermusic.com.

[8] "Wonderful Is Your Name," Author Hezekiah Walker, © 1999.

Scripts:

Call to Worship

Today we begin delving into Money Matters. Now, what does money have to do with faith and worship? you may ask. That's the very same issue that came up the day Jesus was approached by a young man with a burning question: "Teacher" he asked, "what good thing must I do to get eternal life?"

"First," Jesus said, *"only God is truly good. And so if you want to enter real life with God, you must do what God tells you." "What in particular?" the man inquired.*

Jesus replied, "Do not murder, commit adultery, do not steal or lie. Honor your father and mother and love your neighbor as much as you love yourself."

The young man said, "I've done all that; what's left?"

Jesus responded, "If you truly want life to the full, go sell your possessions; give everything to the poor. All your wealth will then be in heaven. Then come follow me."

That was the last thing the young man expected to hear. And sadly, he walked away. He was holding on tight to a lot of things and couldn't bear to let go.

There's just something about how we handle our money that uncovers the core of who we are, the true faith that is inside us. And today we hear the call of Jesus to full DEVOTION, to offer up all we have and all we are to the One who can fully care for us. As we begin our worship today, hear this song of "Total Praise" and give your heart to the one who calls you.

Updates

Each year during this series on Money Matters we try our best to come around the real needs of people, and are offering a **Get Out of Debt For Good** class every Sunday at 11:30 AM for three weeks. This is a non-threatening way to step out of the financial bondage that can easily weigh us down. Everyone is welcome—details in your bulletin.

Each week we've shown you a glimpse of Sudan, video clips from the August trip when our pastor and team traveled to discover all they could about the people and their needs. This week we have for you now a **Miracle Minute** countdown. Let's watch. (*Sudan Miracle Minute Video*)

We give our offerings to recognize God's faithfulness in our lives, and the promise to be faithful through us in the lives of others, both close to home and far away. Let's give with grateful hearts to this song of joy.

MONEY MATTER$ MESSAGE OUTLINE: DEVOTION[9]
Matthew 19:16-26

    A. Courage to Live Truly

        1. Eternal life   (29:16)

        2. Perfect and complete   (29: 21)

    B. Courage to Let Go

        1. Deal with the fear

        2. A good God

    C. Courage to Give

        1. God's priority

        2. Economics 101   (Proverbs 19:17, 11:24-25; Malachi 3:10-12)

[9] This message can be viewed or read at
http://ginghamsburg.org/sermonvideo/article/money-matter/

Stewardship Worship Celebration 2: Debt-Free

Series: MONEY MATTER$

Word: 2 Kings 4:1-7

Felt Need: Debt restrains me from being a "player" for God

Desired Outcome: To take tough steps now to be a future provider

Theme: Debt-free

Metaphor/Look: Kids running

Pre-celebration Music	Children's choir Let Us Pray[11]	You Made the Heavens;[10]
Opening Song & Dance	Children's choir	So Good to Me[12]
Call to Worship	Host w/ various children	Freedom Scriptures *See scripts for sample.*
Song Celebration	Leader/children's choir	Hey, Jesus Loves Me[13]; We All Bow Down[14]
Updates/Video	Host	1) Get Out of Debt classes 2) Hotel Rwanda viewing
Offerings Song	Choir/Band	Thank You Lord[15]
Message	Pastor	Money Matter$: DEBT-FREE; *See below for outline.*
Communion	Host intros/Band	Chaplet of the Divine Mercy
Send Out	Pastor or Host	Communion song cont.
Exit Music	Band	TBD

[10] "You made the Heavens," Author Sarah Moore; © Copyright 1998 Sarah Moore, assigned 2000 to Music Precedent, Ltd.
[11] "Let Us Pray," Author Steven Curtis Chapman; © Copyright 1996 Sparrow Song (a div. of EMI Christian Music Publishing); Peach Hill Songs.
[12] "So Good to Me," Authors Darrell Patton Evans and Matt Jones; © Copyright 1998, Integrity's Hosanna! Music.
[13] "Hey, Jesus Loves Me," Authors Jeff Quimby and Steve Merkel; © Copyright 2004, Integrity's Hosanna! Music.
[14] "We All Bow Down," Author Lenny LeBlanc; © Copyright 2002 Integrity's Hosanna! Music, LenSongs Publishing.
[15] "Thank You Lord," Author Don Moen, on D: I Worship (special edition vol. 1); Authors Don Moen and Paul Baloche; © Copyright 2004 Integrity's Hosanna! Music.

Scripts:

Call to Worship

Host: Good evening! Hear these New Testament words of challenge and hope:

Kid 1: Owe no one anything except to love one another.

Kid 2: I cried to the LORD, and he answered by setting me free.

Kid 3: And if the Son sets you free, you will be free indeed.

Kid 4: Stand firm, then, and do not let yourselves be burdened again by a yoke of slavery.

Host: Keep your lives free from the love of money and be content with what you have, because God has said, "Never will I leave you; never will I forsake you."

All begin song "Hey, Jesus Loves You."

Updates

God calls us to freedom in our financial lives. Our **Get Out of Debt For Good** class is offered Sunday and for the next two weeks. No judgment given; practical steps in financial freedom will be offered. Everyone is welcome. More details in your bulletin.

This Tuesday evening the pastor will host a viewing of the movie **Hotel Rwanda,** here in the worship area. Following the film, the pastor will lead a discussion of the impact of that crisis. Come to learn how we can pray and act responsibly.

As you know, our church is deeply involved with the plight of the Sudanese people. We are actively engaged in an agricultural project to relieve hunger and ultimately save precious lives, adults and children who now depend on us. As the Kidz On Da Rock share this song, we give our offerings and see the faces of the very children we seek to help. Let God speak to your heart now as we give our offerings.

MONEY MATTER$ MESSAGE OUTLINE: DEBT-FREE[16]

2 Kings 4:1-7

    A. Prepare for God's Promised Future

        1. Prepare for the unexpected

        2. Position children for success   (Proverbs 13:22)

        3. Provide for God's blessing to others   (Romans 13:8)

    B. Use What You Have in Your House

        1. Contentment   (1 Timothy 2:6-8)

        2. Delayed gratification   (James 1:4)

        3. Expectation

        4. Seek the support of community

    C. Keep Pouring

        1. The gift of work   (Colossians 3:23)

        2. Maximize your opportunity

---

[16] This message can be viewed or read at
http://ginghamsburg.org/sermonvideo/article/money-matter-debt-free/

Stewardship Worship Celebration 3: Discipline

Series: MONEY MATTER$

Word: Matthew 25:14-30

Felt Need: Financial/life freedom

Desired Outcome: Discipline that leads to freedom

Theme: Discipline: faithful—fruitful—fearless

Metaphor/Look: Bag of coins

Gathering Music	Band	Jazz Vibe
Call to Worship/ Storytelling Skit	Storyteller w/3 players	Matthew 25
Song Celebration		Freedom Scriptures
Song Celebration	Band	Ain't No Rock[17]
Updates/Video	Host w/ Board Member	
Offerings/Feature Song	Band	Let That Be Enough[18]
Message	Pastor	Money Matter$: DISCIPLINE *See below for outline.*
Response/Send Out	Host	TBD
Exit Music	Band	Once Again[19]

[17] "Ain't No Rock," CCLI Song Number 614055; Author LaMarquis Jefferson; ©Copyright 1987, Integrity's Praise! Music.

[18] "Let That Be Enough," CCLI Song Number 2812982; Author Jonathan Foreman; © Copyright 1999, Meadowgreen Music Company (Admin. by EMI Christian Music Publishing); Sugar Pete Songs (Admin. by EMI Christian Music Publishing).

[19] "Once Again," CCLI Song Number 1564362; Author Matt Redman; © Copyright 1995, Thankyou Music (Admin. by EMI Christian Music Publishing).

Call To Worship/Storytelling Skit from Matthew 25

(as Players enter worship area and begin to walk towards the stage on floor, one at a time) Today we open with a parable from the Gospel of Matthew, the story of a business owner of some means going off on an extended trip. Before she left, she called her servants together and entrusted her property to them. To one she gave five thousand dollars, to another two thousand, to a third one thousand, depending on their abilities. *(One by one the Players receive their money.)* Then she went on her journey. *(Storyteller steps forward as Players walk behind her to Storyteller's left and turn away from audience, animatedly "dealing" w/their money in the manner that Storyteller describes. Players remain turned away from audience, but moving continuously, each one "dealing" with their money in their respective ways.)*

After a long time the master of those servants returned and settled accounts with them. *(Storyteller backs up to original spot.)* The woman who had received the five thousand dollars *(Player 1 excitedly waves her doubled money at Storyteller.)* showed her how she had doubled her investment. Her master commended her: "Good work! You did your job well! You have been faithful with this much; I will put you in charge of much more. From now on, be my partner." *(Player 1 crosses and stands proudly to Storyteller's right.)*

The servant with the two thousand *(Player 2 excitedly waves his doubled money at Storyteller.)* showed how he also had doubled his master's investment. His master commended him: "Good work! You did your job well. From now on you'll be my partner as well." *(Player 2 is beside himself with pride and crosses over to stand at Storyteller's right, next to Player 1.)*

Then the man who had received the one thousand *(Player 3 approaches Storyteller with a prideful attitude, thinking he's done the right thing)* said, "Master, I know you have high standards and hate careless ways, and that you demand the best and make no allowances for error. I was afraid I might disappoint you, so I found a good hiding place for your money. Here it is, safe and sound, down to the last cent!" *(Player 3 pulls the money out of a hidden pocket, very dramatically.)*

The master was furious! "That's a terrible way to live! *(Player 3 slowly begins to shrink and cower during this lecture.)* It's criminal to live fearfully! If you knew I was after the best, why didn't you do your part? You should have at least invested it at the bank so I would have gotten a little interest. Take the thousand and give it to the one who risked the most without fear *(Player 3 sadly crosses over in front of Storyteller and gives his money to Player 1...)* and lose the play-it-safe attitudes! For everyone who has will be given more, and he or she will have more than enough. (Thank you, servants!) *(Players exit stage ext. to right as audience applauds.)*

(Storyteller continues to audience) Financial freedom is not about how much we have, rather about the discipline to be faithful, fruitful, and fearless *(main graphic)* with what we've been given . . . and when we're faithful, God always provides More Than Enough. Today we've come to give our best to that generous and amazing God. Let's get started as we worship together.

Updates

Welcome! Our hearts are in many places this morning. Two teams have recently returned from doing great work at the Hurricane Katrina site. We'll be hearing about more opportunities for mission to that area in months to come. Our project in the Sudan has God's hand all over it, and we will be hearing more on that in the upcoming weeks. Since the holidays are just around the corner we are excited to have for you our own customized Christmas Cards that feature the heart of Jesus for the poor, and offer information on back for how the recipient can be involved as well. These boxed sets will be available next weekend. Spread the word as we all spread some hope this Christmas.

Right now one of our Leadership Board servants is coming with a message for you.

Board Member: Thanks. I don't know about you, but this series on Money Matters has really spoken to me. We've heard how financial freedom begins with heart devotion, ultimately leads to obedience in regular giving, in creating a budget as well as in getting out of the slavery of debt. This week in the mail church attendees will receive a letter from our Pastor calling us to commitment. God's people have always been called to hear God's call and then act on what God has said. In this letter you'll find a sample of the commitment cards we'll receive next week in worship. Prayerfully look the sample card over, and listen to what God is asking you to do. If you have questions, you are welcome to call our stewardship officer here at the church. (show phone no.) Next week, we'll have a celebration of Thanksgiving, stories of hope and a time to offer our commitment to God, thanking God ahead of time for providing More Than Enough.

We want to give our offerings to God now. I serve in the recovery celebration here at the church, and I know from experience how easy it is to think that we need something MORE to fill the empty places in our lives. As we give our offerings, hear this prayer of devotion, for God's presence and provision are truly enough.

24 "I'll Trust You Lord," Author Donnie McClurkin; Don Mac Music, Seven Summits Music

MONEY MATTER$ MESSAGE: DISCIPLINE
Matthew 25:14-30

    A.   Faithful   (25:14-15)

        1. The issue of ownership   (1 Corinthians 4:2)
        2. Trust and greater responsibility   (Luke 16:11, Malachi 3:10)

    B. Fruitful   (25:16)

        1. Planting seeds   (Proverbs 30:25)
        2. Working the harvest
          "well done"   (Proverbs 22:29)

    C. Fearless   (25:25)

        1. Paralysis of fear
        2. Activate faith   (1 Corinthians 16:2)

Stewardship Worship Celebration 4: More Than Enough

Series: MONEY MATTER$

Word: Malachi 3:10-11

Felt Need: I need hope and provision—
God needs my trust and praise

Desired Outcome: Commit my best/celebrate
God's provision

Theme: More Than Enough

Metaphor/Look: Hands overflowing with grain

Opening Music	Band/Gospel Choir	I've Got A Testimony[20]
Welcome/ Call to Worship	Host	*See script for sample.*
Song Celebration	Band/Gospel Choir	I Will Bless the Lord;[21] Give Thanks;[22] Amazing Grace[23]
Message Segment	Cohosts	Video Story #1—Darren and Tammy Video Story #2—Joe and Val
Personal Words/ Card Explanation	Leader of the Board	*See script for sample*
Reflection Time/ Offerings	Band	I'll Trust You Lord[24]
Send Out	Pastor or Host	
Exit Music	Band	I Will Bless the Lord

---

[20] "I've Got a Testimony," CCLI Song Number 2844833; Author Anthony Tidewell; © Copyright 1995, Meek Gospel Music (Admin. by Meek Recording & Publishing Company, Inc.).

[21] "I Will Bless the Lord," CCLI Song Number 3262184; Author Joseph, II Pace; © Copyright 2001 Integrity's Praise! Music; Pace's Vision Music (Admin. by Integrity Music, Inc.).

[22] "Give Thanks," CCLI Song Number 20285; Author Henry Smith; © Copyright 1978 Integrity's Hosanna! Music.

[23] Public domain

[24] "I'll Trust You Lord," Author Donnie McClurkin; Don Mac Music, Seven Summits Music.

Scripts:
Call To Worship

Good evening/morning! Do you have a testimony? If you don't have one already, hang on. Here's our Scripture for tonight/today from Malachi 3: *"Bring the whole tithe, a tenth of all you earn, into the storehouse, that there may be food in my house.*

And test me in this, says the LORD Almighty, see if I will not throw open the floodgates of heaven and pour out so much blessing that you will have MORE THAN ENOUGH!"

Tonight/today we come to hear God's call for a life-practice that may not make sense to us. It's a call to commit to God a portion of what we have and make, then to watch as God turns that trust into amazing provision. This is a God who takes care of God's children. This is a God who generously supplies everything we need and then some. This is the God we've come to worship and celebrate. Stand and join us as we bless the Lord!

MORE
THAN ENOUGH

giving period:
january 1 - december 31,_____

name:_____
address:_____
city, state, zip:_____
Phone:_____

OUR MISSION:

❏ YES! I will pray for our mission and ministry in this place. I estimate I will grow in my giving to the mission here at _____ Church next year as follows:

My yearly commitment to general funds and missions is $_____.
I plan to pay it as follows:

$_____Weekly $_____monthly
$_____quarterly $_____annually

❏ This represents an increase over what I am giving in $_____.

❏ I am interested in the automatic bank draft method of payment. (you will be contacted for specific information.)

❏ I Would like to receive my giving statements via E-mail. Please send my statement to:_____

I understand this estimate of giving may be revised or cancelled at any time at my request.

Source file for this commitment card can be found on the DVD.

Commitment Cards (Board Member Testimony)

For those of you that have been here over the past month, you may remember that our Money Matters series began with the story about the rich young ruler that was doing everything right in his life but wanted more. When Jesus told him to sell his possessions and give the money to the poor, he walked away dejected because he could not do that.

How we handle our money says so much about us. When God promises us great blessings in return for our tithe as in Malachi 3 (**"I will pour out a blessing so great you won't have enough room to take it in."**) and we don't have the faith to do it, we are missing out on guaranteed blessings from a God that tells us to TEST HIM! ... Malachi 3:10

Nineteen years ago I was spiritually, physically, mentally, and financially bankrupt. I had made some poor decisions and an addiction problem took me to my knees, almost killed me, and it nearly destroyed my family. But, by the grace of God I was saved, I asked God to deliver me from this hell, and God did. As a part of our transformation process, my wife and I decided that we had needed to become regular "givers" to God. He had saved my life and our family, and we felt as though it was the least we could do and we were up for anything. And maybe, just maybe he would bless us even more, just like it says in the Bible ... we were in some ways "testing him."

The Bible asks us to tithe, and what a tough thing that was for us. We had huge credit card debt, a mortgage to pay, as well as a car payment. Because of my problems, I could only work part time and was facing jail time. The numbers did not add up when thinking about adding a "tithe" to our expenses. This is when we acted on faith and said we were going to do it anyway.

How many times in the Bible do things not add up? Remember when Jesus fed 5,000 people with 5 loaves of bread and 2 fish and had bread to spare?

Some 19 years later my wife and I look back in amazement at the many ways that God has blessed us. I don't want it to sound like our life has been perfect. We've had heartache and trials and tribulations, but the blessings have outnumbered all of these trials many times over.

Our tithe is no longer considered an "expense." It is a faithful commitment to a God that loved us so much that God would take numbers that didn't add up and not only make them add up, but add to them exponentially. I am so glad that we decided to "test" God.

You have your commitment cards[25] in front of you. The card says "More Than Enough," and we know from the stories we have heard today that our God will always provide more than enough if we are faithful servants.

It is time to put your faith into action. Please take a moment to prayerfully discern what God is telling you to commit to. Discernment is asking God what to give. This allows you to give what God is blessing rather than asking God to bless what you are doing.

Some of you are visiting here or you are still trying to sort this whole commitment thing out. This is not for you—and that is okay. This is for people who acknowledge that Jesus Christ is Lord. Everyone needs to step up from wherever you have been.

Take a look at what the chart for personal plan for commitment[25] says. This chart has various levels of income and what you would need to give in order to reach a certain percentage of giving.

Figure out where you are at. If you are giving nothing, consider starting somewhere. If you only give when you attend, then make a commitment to give weekly whether you attend church or not.

If you are currently tithing your net income, God may be asking you to tithe your gross income. God may even be speaking to you about going above and beyond the regular tithe this year. Wherever you are, listen and act in faith.

Please fill out the card completely and check the box if this new commitment represents an increase over last year. Also make sure you check the applicable boxes if you are interested in automatic bank draft or if you would like to receive your giving statements via email for your convenience.

> It is not until you are able to give something away that God will trust you with more, and when you faithfully give it away God will trust you with ... MORE THAN ENOUGH.

We will take a few moments of reflective time now to complete the cards. *(soft music begins)*

Reflection time to complete commitment cards

Let's give our offerings now and place our cards in the offering baskets as well. God bless you.

---

[25] Art for this card can be found on the DVD if you open the file from a computer's DVD drive. The art is in Adobe Photoshop format and may be customized, then duplicated in quantities to meet your needs.

Updates

May God bless this time and your trust into the year ahead. We've enjoyed a time of celebration, we've committed ourselves to God's call, and now we want to turn a corner into our challenge for the next month, our Advent season. As you know, we have followed the call of Jesus and committed our financial resources towards a huge project to feed and provide development for thousands of men, women, and children. We've accepted the challenge to make this a simpler Christmas in our homes, enjoying the presence *of* one another rather than presents *from* one another. We've created Christmas cards to lift up the Sudan project and they are available for purchase now in the bookstore for you to spread the hope and heart of Jesus in this season.

In addition we have the informational gift cards for you to take that articulate to friends and family the reason for your simple Christmas plans. As we come closer to Christmas we realize this is a miracle of biblical proportions that God is working through the people of our church. Watch now as we join hearts for this project. *(Sudan Project Video)*

Send Out

It's time for a change, to assure that all of God's children have MORE THAN ENOUGH, and we want to be part of that change. Go this week in the fresh commitment you have made to the mission of Jesus in the world. Amen.

"Getting Out of Debt For Good" classes are very important to a year-round stewardship emphasis. Start some classes now and order enough copies of *Money Matters: Financial Freedom for All God's Children*. ISBN: 0687495350.

Chapter Five

Group Study Companion

Money Matters: Financial Freedom for All God's Children

The mission of Jesus is liberation. He came to free individuals and communities from all forms of oppression. Carefully planned group Bible studies, formed around individuals' felt needs, providing practical information as well as meaningful participation, can be the most powerful tool for transformation in the congregation. In more than twenty-five years of pastoral leadership, I have found this group study on Money Matters to be one of the most life-changing offerings that we make for the people of our congregation.

These weekly group studies are a resource for you to use in your setting, designed for both class and cell group settings. Each week's study coincides with a chapter from the companion book, *Money Matters: Financial Freedom for All God's Children* (ISBN: 0687495350 Abingdon Press, 2006). Participants should read the related chapters weekly as a preparation for the group study.

My intention is for you to use this resource to lead a group of leaders who will then be equipped to teach others. Ultimately, these principles have the power to spread throughout your church and beyond, allowing God to use your faith community as a force for Jesus' liberating mission in the world.

Images for these group studies can be found in a folder on the DVD, which is viewable on a computer hard drive. These images are primarily intended for projection during worship celebrations, but they can also be imported into PowerPoint if the teacher has an interest in projecting the structure of the study, or if the group is large. With groups larger than twelve persons, however, it is difficult to get honest sharing about personal choices with spending, saving, and giving. Self-critical honesty is essential to accountability, which results in changed behavior.

Week 1—A Faith-filled Focus

Greet and get acquainted with each person in the group.

Open in prayer.

Read this Scripture together, by asking someone to read it out loud:

1 Timothy 6:17-19
Command those who are rich in this present world not to be arrogant nor to put their hope in wealth, which is so uncertain, but to put their hope in God, who richly provides us with everything for our enjoyment. Command them to do good, to be rich in good deeds, and to be generous and willing to share. In this way they will lay up treasure for themselves as a firm foundation for the coming age, so that they may take hold of the life that is truly life.

Group Discussion Question: Why are you here today?
The goal of this study is to learn and encourage one another to "put our hope in God" as Timothy says (above). More specifically, what is *your* Money Matter today?

A Powerful Parent

Read together Matthew 7:7-11: *Ask and you will receive; seek and you will find; knock and the door will be opened. Which of you, if your child asks for bread, will give him a stone? Or if a child asks for fish, will give him a snake? If you then, who are evil, know how to give good gifts to your children, how much more will your father in heaven give good things to those who ask him.*

Ask each person to identify and write/journal his or her responses (share together if desired):
1. Consider your earthly parents. In regards to care and provision, how were they similar or different than your powerful heavenly parent?
2. Do you truly believe that "there is nothing you can do to change God's love, no matter how badly you mess up"? Financial freedom will come only as we accept God's love, care and provision for us as God's children. If you don't trust God's unconditional love, it will be difficult to trust God's provision.

The Promise of Provision

Teach: Life is not about frantically pursuing money and possessions, because God has already promised all we need. Life is about pursuing a relationship with God through Jesus Christ. We begin to build a lifetime of financial freedom by readjusting our priorities. Jesus put it this way: *"Seek first the kingdom of God and his righteousness and everything else will be added unto you"* (Matthew 6:33).

Ask each person to:
1. List your current priorities, the top ten things that always get your attention each week.
2. Write down a specific way you would like to re-prioritize your life, putting "the Kingdom of God and his righteousness" first on the list. What about your life will have to change this very week?

The Principle of Biblical Prosperity

Teach: As Christians we still make the mistake of thinking we're going to be blessed just because we're under the blood of Jesus Christ. Instead, we must submit ourselves to all of the laws and principles of God.

Read together Ephesians 5:17: *"Don't be foolish but understand what the will of the Lord is."*

Ask each person to:
1. Name foolish financial mistakes that you have made in your life. (This is not easy to do for some persons, so ask persons to write it down privately, and then ask for volunteers to share what they can. Be careful to watch for and prevent anger or blaming behavior, since vocalizing of anger or blame is better left for personal counseling, and the pain may involve another person in the group.)
2. How have you been unrealistic in your financial matters? Have you expected God to provide even when you've made foolish decisions or simply ignored God's financial principles?

Today Is the Day

Teach: We must declare that *today* is the day of our salvation and keep a focus of heart devotion.

Our ultimate financial freedom from God will be directly proportionate to how badly we want it and how willing we are to take the necessary steps. **Name** out loud what it is that you hear God asking you to start doing this week. **Ask** the others in the group to hold you accountable.

Close in prayer, asking God to strengthen each person to take his or her first difficult steps towards financial freedom.

Week 2—Devoted to Our Rightful Owner

Welcome one another and introduce any new persons to the group.

Ask how the week went and give each person time to state how they were or were not successful at following through with the steps from last week. Do not spend too much time here, rather build on the best, and determine to keep moving forward. Guard against allowing this time of study to become a financial counseling session for any one person. Keep the focus on those who are diligently doing the work and the new principles God is naming for each person.

A Series of Conversions

We have been born again and have all the resources of the Spirit in our lives, but the resources cannot be released until we are converted. Conversion in our finances means we will change our thinking and practice to the thinking and practice of Jesus.

Ask and allow time for responses:
1. Think back and identify the time when you named Jesus as Lord. Does this study of personal financial habits (and the steps you are now taking) hold the same importance and expectation as your initial conversion to Jesus?
2. Are you ready to take more steps this week to find freedom, and allow God's resources to be released? (If the group is too large for each individual to respond, consider designating discussion "partners" for group question discussion.)

The Recognition of Rightful Ownership

Read together Exodus 4:1-4:
> Moses answered, "What if they do not believe me or listen to me and say, 'The LORD did not appear to you'?"
> Then the LORD said to him, "What is that in your hand?"
> "A staff," he replied.
> The LORD said, "Throw it on the ground."
> Moses threw it on the ground and it became a snake, and he ran from it. Then the LORD said to him, "Reach out your hand and take it by the tail." So Moses reached out and took hold of the snake and it turned back into a staff in his hand.

Ask/Write down: You already have "in your hand" everything you need for financial freedom. Make a list of five assets, talents, traits, or experiences that could possibly show financial value if given to God and used well.

The Responsibility of Trust

Teach: God isn't calling you to release what you *don't* have; God is calling you to release what you *do* have.

Ask: 1. "What we don't have" is often represented by our use of credit. Why do you find it so hard to trust God's provision rather than using credit cards and borrowing?
2. Consider a prayer of trust, releasing to God everything you own, the people you are close to, and the assets God's given to you personally. Make a list of what you have given to God. You may need to remember this prayer of trust later on in your journey!

Belief vs. Faith

"Many people say they believe in Jesus and they profess Jesus, but they put trust for their security and meaning in their physical possessions—from their money."

Group Discussion ... Think about what you've learned in these first two chapters. How does your "worldview" need to be transformed to the world-view of Jesus?

Choose one of the statements below to describe your current need:
1. I need to see God as rightful owner of my life and possessions.
2. I must deal with my debt, so I can be more present to the needs of others.
3. I must "release" something to God that feels difficult for me to let go.

Read together Proverbs 22:4, *"Humility and the fear of the LORD bring wealth and honor and life."*

View the "Jay and Lori" digital story together, which is found on the DVD companion that is bound into this book for leaders. The story can be found on the DVD in the section: "Money Matters, Stories Of Faith and Freedom."

In closing allow each person to express in **prayer** what he or she is hearing God say. This can be spoken or written down. Some may wish to ask the others to pray for them.

Week 3—Surrender, Trust, and Freedom

Welcome the group.

Ask what initial insights or "light bulb moments" anyone might have had from reading Chapter 3 that week. Keep this opening discussion brief and moving forward.

Read together 1 Kings 17:7-14:

> Some time later the brook dried up because there had been no rain in the land. Then the word of the LORD came to Elijah: "Go at once to Zarephath of Sidon and stay there. I have commanded a widow in that place to supply you with food."
>
> So he went to Zarephath. When he came to the town gate, a widow was there gathering sticks. He called to her and asked, "Would you bring me a little water in a jar so I may have a drink?" As she was going to get it, he called, "And bring me, please, a piece of bread."
>
> "As surely as the LORD your God lives," she replied, "I don't have any bread—only a handful of flour in a jar and a little oil in a jug. I am gathering a few sticks to take home and make a meal for myself and my son, that we may eat it—and die."
>
> Elijah said to her, "Don't be afraid. Go home and do as you have said. But first make a small cake of bread for me from what you have and bring it to me, and then make something for yourself and your son. For this is what the LORD, the God of Israel, says: 'The jar of flour will not be used up and the jug of oil will not run dry until the day the LORD gives rain on the land.'"

Teach: The widow in this story from 1 Kings could only see what she did not have. She used the formula of human computation, and she was unaware of the power of divine math.

Ask each person to answer these questions, either out loud or silently:
  1. When considering your life and provisions each day, are you more likely to think about what you *do* have or what you *don't* have?
  2. Name a time in your life that "divine math" took over and, although it didn't make sense at the time, God's provision was miraculous.

Discipline and Delayed Gratification

Teach: Two life practices that are essential for financial freedom are discipline and delayed gratification. The result will be Christ-like character in our lives. Our use of credit, however, prohibits God from developing these characteristics in our lives.

View together the "Lance and Amber" story from the DVD companion that is bound with this book, in the section, "Money Matters, Stories of Faith and Freedom."

When Lance and Amber realized how their accumulation of debt had enslaved them, they were able to exercise great discipline and delayed gratification in order to obtain their higher goal of financial freedom.

Ask:
1. How strong is your discipline "muscle"?
2. How strong is your delayed gratification "muscle"?
3. What are you hearing God say?

Think and Act: The widow of Zarephath was open and honest with Elijah. Do you need to confide in a financial mentor or accountability partner(s) in order to gain significant strength for these "muscles"?

Close in prayer.

Week 4—Stewardship 101

Welcome the group.

Open with prayer for God's presence and power in the group time.

Discuss as a group: do you believe the following statement?

"The effectiveness of your life is not found in what you own, but in the stewardship of what you've been given. You have everything you need to start right now fulfilling God's purpose in your life and to ultimately achieve financial health."

Read together 1 Samuel 17:38-40. Focus particularly on *vv.* 38-39:
> *Saul dressed David in his own (Saul's) tunic. He put a coat of armor on him and a bronze helmet on his head. David fastened on his sword over the tunic and tried walking around, because he was not used to them.*
> *"I cannot go in these," David said to Saul, "because I am not used to them." So he took them off. Then he took his staff in his hand, chose five smooth stones from the stream, put them in the pouch of his shepherd's bag and, with his sling in his hand, approached the Philistine.*

Teach: David's success in his career-launching battle with Goliath was not found in someone else's closet but rather in what was already in his possession, the sling and stones.

Ask: 1. How has your financial situation been adversely affected by the false belief that you need what someone else possesses in order to be happy?
2. What skill has God given you that you must faithfully use to realize God's provision?

Dealing with Debt

Read Proverbs 22:7: *"Just as the rich rule the poor, so the borrower is servant to the lender."*

Teach: We must think of ourselves as God's investment partners rather than as people of need.

Jesus died to set you free, but as long as you owe even a dollar to someone you will always be a slave to that person and be unable to assume the role of God's investment partner. Remember, getting out of debt is hard work. It is a commitment. It begins with plastic surgery, cutting up those credit cards, which is an act of faith. In faith we depend on God instead of Visa or MasterCard for our needs.

View the DVD segments entitled, "How Are You Getting Out of Debt?" located on the DVD companion to this book.

Ask: What ideas do these story segments give you regarding ways you can reduce and eliminate your own debt?

Discipline and Christ-like Character

Read: Matthew 6:21: *"For where your treasure is, there your heart will be also."*

Teach: You are being prepared for eternity, and God is currently building that enduring Christ-like character in you. Christ-like character comes through discipline and discipline begins in the area of our finances and possessions. It doesn't matter how much or how little we have, it's living within the means of what we have. Simply put, discipline in finances requires a budget.

Discuss and decide: Make sure that everyone understands the simple 10-10-80 structure for getting started on a budget:
   10% of income to God
   10% of income to the future (savings/investment/retirement)
   80% of income to living expenses

Homework:

It doesn't matter how much or how little we have, it's living within the means of what we have.

If anyone in the group does not currently have a working budget, this week's homework is to create one. Start by writing down all mandatory expenses. Create categories for everything needed and place realistic amounts per month on each category. Get in the habit of recording each expenditure or use the simple "envelope method," described in Chapter 4 of *Money Matters: Financial Freedom for All God's Children.* (Tip: Most persons have a computer spreadsheet program at home, such as Microsoft Excel. If your class is unlikely to use such a program, ruled paper will work fine.)

If anyone in the group needs further assistance in budget-making, assign them to a partner or create a class just for this exercise in living within their means. Budgeting is an essential step, regardless of income level!

Closing: Action Steps

Confess to one another where you've been and commit to where you're going.

1. What are some of the foolish decisions you have made in the past concerning financial purchases?
2. What new decisions are you making that will prevent you from repeating these mistakes?

Week 5—Living Debt-free

Welcome the group.

Read Romans 13:8: *"Let no debt remain outstanding, except the continuing debt to love one another, for whoever loves others has fulfilled the law."*

View the DVD story, "I Wanna Be Rich" on the DVD companion to this book.

Teach: Debt mortgages our future to the past, but there is good news: We don't have to stay there. Jesus came to liberate us. Faith in God requires obedient action. When you're willing to obey and pay the cost with your best, God meets you with God's best. The first step in becoming or staying debt free is to prepare yourself for what God wants to do with you and your possessions. This includes: preparing for the unexpected, putting our children in a position of success, and beginning to become the hands and feet of Jesus by providing God's blessing to others in need.

Describe to one another:
  1. A time that an unexpected event caused you to go into debt.
  2. A time when you were able to provide a financial or material blessing to another person. How did that make you feel?

Teach: Debt occurs when we attempt to fill the empty places in our life with things instead of God. It is when we begin to trust and rely on God that we become content with how God has already blessed us, and patient as we trust in God for our needs.

View two stories of faith and freedom from the DVD companion:
The Randy and Kathi story, then the Darren and Tammy story

Review together the "Six Steps to Getting Out of Debt for Good" from Chapter 5 of *Money Matters: Financial Freedom for All God's Children*. Identify where you are in those steps and share with the group:
  1. Your next step in becoming debt-free.
  2. When you will begin taking that step?

Pray for one another and in closing, ask all persons to bring evidence of the hard work they'll do in the coming week toward achieving financial freedom. Share these pieces of evidence next week.

Week 6—Creators vs. Consumers

Welcome each person and one by one share the "evidence" of the hard work each one has brought, demonstration of work done towards achieving financial freedom.

Read together 2 Kings 4:1-7:

> The wife of a man from the company of the prophets cried out to Elisha, "Your servant my husband is dead, and you know that he revered the LORD. But now his creditor is coming to take my two boys as his slaves."
>
> Elisha replied to her, "How can I help you? Tell me, what do you have in your house?"
>
> "Your servant has nothing there at all," she said, "except a little olive oil."
>
> Elisha said, "Go around and ask all your neighbors for empty jars. Don't ask for just a few. Then go inside and shut the door behind you and your sons. Pour oil into all the jars, and as each is filled, put it to one side."She left him and shut the door behind her and her sons. They brought the jars to her and she kept pouring. When all the jars were full, she said to her son,"Bring me another one."
>
> But he replied, "There is not a jar left." Then the oil stopped flowing.
>
> She went and told the man of God, and he said, "Go, sell the oil and pay your debts. You and your sons can live on what is left."

Faithfully Live

Teach: The single mother in the 2 Kings story discovered that she would need to "create more than she consumed or she would cease to exist." Translated to today, we must make more than we spend, and continually make wise decisions in our money matters, lest our quality of life and influence be greatly diminished.

You already have all the gifts, all the talents, and all the resources you need within you to build a basis for financial freedom. God has wired you to be a creator, not a consumer, using those talents and resources wisely and without fear.

Reflect out loud or silently:

1. Since God has wired you to be a creator rather than simply a consumer, how does that change your attitude regarding work, possessions, and relationships?

2. At the present, would you say you are a giver or a taker when it comes to money, possessions and emotional energy? How would you like to change?

Faithfully Work

Teach: Of all the creatures that God created; you are created in the image of God. It doesn't mean that you physically look like God; rather, that you also have the ability to create. Unlike any other creature, you have the ability to conceive something in your mind and then put it to work.

View: Maria's story, "Working Woman," from the DVD companion to this book.

Ask:
1. How is Maria's story like the single mother in 2 Kings?
2. What about Maria's story do you like the most?
3. What are you inspired to do as a result of seeing Maria's story?

Faithfully Invest

Teach: Everything you need you already have. Now you must work the "package" that God has given you.

List your "package assets." These are the gifts, talents, and resources you uniquely possess. Is there a way you might "put out more jars," inviting God to use your assets/package in a greater way for more return on your investment?

Strategic Partnerships

Challenge: You must maximize your potential by finding strategic partnerships. Look for those persons who are a little ahead of you, or who are gifted in areas that you aren't. Ask if you can pick their brain, shadow behind them, or meet to discuss your best next steps. Watch God work as you take these essential steps toward freedom.

Close in prayer for faith and discipline to continue on the journey to financial freedom.

Week 7—Lifestyles of the Disciplined and Generous

Welcome one another.

Teach: Generous giving is a different kind of practice, an expression of your heart, rather than a rational cerebral action. Heart is most closely connected to spirit. When you live by the Spirit, there's something about giving that just feels "right."

Ask: 1. Name someone you know who has demonstrated great financial generosity. Why do you think they were/are motivated to give?
2. If giving feels so "right," then why is it still hard for us to do?

Read Luke 9:10-17.

> When the apostles returned, they reported to Jesus what they had done. Then he took them with him and they withdrew by themselves to a town called Bethsaida, but the crowds learned about it and followed him. He welcomed them and spoke to them about the kingdom of God, and healed those who needed healing.
>
> Late in the afternoon the Twelve came to him and said, "Send the crowd away so they can go to the surrounding villages and countryside and find food and lodging, because we are in a remote place here."
>
> He replied, "You give them something to eat."
>
> They answered, "We have only five loaves of bread and two fish—unless we go and buy food for this crowd." (About five thousand men were there.)
>
> But he said to his disciples, "Have them sit down in groups of about fifty each." The disciples did so, and everybody sat down. Taking the five loaves and the two fish and looking up to heaven, he gave thanks and broke them. Then he gave them to the disciples to set before the people. They all ate and were satisfied, and the disciples picked up twelve basketfuls of broken pieces that were left over.

Teach: The disciples suffered from a "limitation theology," thinking that what they could see was all they had. Most of us have this same mindset.

Discuss: (as it relates to the story from Luke 9 above).

"The act of generous giving activates the law of miraculous multiplication."

The Nature of God

Teach: Generosity is the nature of God. *"For God so loved the world that he gave his only son."* You can't have love without generosity. Love, in its purest form, is the act of generous, sacrificial giving. Whenever consumption exceeds generosity it is not love, but lust.

Ask: 1. How have you confused love with lust?
2. Giving financially sets our "love" in motion. Do you hear God calling you to a new place of "giving" love?

The Love of God

Read Matthew 6:21: *"For where your treasure is, there your heart will be also."*

Teach: Generosity is the expression of our love for God. Generous giving is an act of worship. Financial freedom is not about the love of money; it's about the love of God, how you worship, and where you put your treasure. The Bible calls this the principle of the tithe.

Ask: How does this explanation of the "tithe" differ from an earlier understanding of the tithe that you may have had?

Read Malachi 3:8-11: *Will anyone rob God? Yet you are robbing me! But you say, "How are we robbing you?" In your tithes and offerings! You are cursed with a curse, for you are robbing me—the whole nation of you! Bring the full tithe into the storehouse, so that there may be food in my house, and thus put me to the test, says the LORD of hosts; see if I will not open the windows of heaven for you and pour down for you an overflowing blessing.*

Teach: A tithe is the first 10 percent, and an offering is anything above the first 10 percent. That is not to discourage the person who has two cents to give. You give what you have, but a tithe is the first 10 percent, and an offering is anything above that 10 percent. *"Bring the full tithe into the storehouse."* What is the storehouse? At the time of this writing by the prophet, it was the Temple. Then it became the synagogue in the Jewish tradition, and for Christians, the house of worship is our church. *"Bring the full tithe into my storehouse so there may be food in my house for the economy of God."* Why is that so strategic? Because we can do more together as faith communities to honor God and bless others (the poor, the hurt, and the oppressed) than any of us could do alone.

Discuss: 1. How is the church, your church, akin to a modern-day storehouse?
2. Why is it imperative that God's people bring the full tithe into this modern-day storehouse, the church?
3. What releases the law of miraculous provision, such as we see with the loaves and fish? (Our tithes and offerings open the floodgates of heaven when we live out the law of generous giving.)

The Provision of God

Ask: Put yourself in the crowd that day when Jesus brought about the miracle of the loaves and fishes. Not yet knowing the miraculous outcome, would you have been willing to give up your lunch that day on the hillside?

Teach: Jesus isn't going to do something from nothing. Jesus needs your lunch. You must risk trusting God with what you have, and that's why giving is an act of worship. We can say we believe in God, but we don't truly trust God until we make an action of faith.

View: the Joe and Val story of God's provision from DVD companion.

When we continue to bless other people, God blesses us more so that we can continue to bless more people. God is amazing. What we give doesn't come back in the same quantity. It's like a yoyo. You can't really get rid of this thing, yet it comes back in a larger quantity than when it left. Jesus says, *"Give and it will be given to you. A good measure, pressed down, shaken together and running over, will be poured in your lap. For the measure you give will be the measure you get back"* (Luke 6:38). We find the same idea in 2 Corinthians 9:6, *"Whoever sows sparingly will also reap sparingly, and whoever sows generously will also reap generously."* The poor have a place of prominence for God's blessing.

Action Steps:
1. Set aside money for giving: 1 Corinthians 16:2, *"On the first day of every week, each one of you should set aside a sum of money in keeping with his income, saving it up, so that when I come no collections will have to be made."*
2. Discipline yourself in giving: 2 Corinthians 8:6, *"Bring also to completion this act of grace on your part."*
3. Base your plan upon God's promises: Deuteronomy 15:10, *"Give generously and the LORD your God will bless you in all your work and in all you undertake."*

Week 8—The Power of Ultimate Sacrifice

Welcome one another, acknowledging that this will be the last official gathering time.

Ask how lives have been affected up to this point. "Conversions" often elicit controversy and may create tension in surrounding relationships. Have new steps toward financial freedom reflected this type of reaction?

The Cost of the Cross

Teach: We must constantly challenge our worldview against the worldview of the Lord Jesus Christ. Everything about life, everything about the purpose of God in our lives, comes back to this cost of the Cross. Jesus knew life wasn't about getting what he wanted and doing his own thing. His purpose was clearly to carry out the mission and purpose of God. God has not placed us here to consume. The meaning of life is found in sacrifice.

Discuss: When you first embarked on the journey toward financial freedom, did you realize it would be such a spiritual experience? How has your relationship with God deepened in this time? Is your life gaining new meaning through sacrifice?

The Call To Commitment

Read Luke 9:24, "*For whoever wants to save their life for themselves will lose it, but whoever wants to lose their life for me will save it.*"

Ask: You can't *lose* your life for Jesus and still keep your hand on it. Are there parts of your old life to which you still cling?

Read: Luke 9:23, "*If any want to become my followers, let them deny themselves and take up their cross daily.*"

Teach: The Call of Jesus is a call to follow. It is a practice of sacrifice every day. This "Jesus thing" is something much bigger than belief. It is following Jesus in the demonstration of sacrifice. Money demonstrates the priority of our values. How we spend it, and what we do with it, tells what we truly believe, no matter what we say with our words.

Ask: What is one specific example of a sacrifice you have made that, although it was painful, you realize it demonstrated what you truly believe?

Recreation and Delayed Gratification

Challenge: Recreation in our lives must never precede or exceed God's mission. This will require us to exercise delayed gratification! If it takes long enough to get something, you forget why you wanted it in the first place, and that is a good thing. If your recreation precedes or exceeds what you are releasing to the mission of Christ, you might believe in Jesus, but you are not following Jesus.

Name something you desire to acquire but realize that you must save ahead for it rather than go into debt over it.

Steps of Commitment

1. Just as Jesus modeled an ultimate commitment on the Cross, resurrection in any area of your life always comes out of sacrifice. Name a specific area in your life that currently requires resurrection. What is the sacrifice you will make in order to allow God to be a powerful life-giver?

2. Recreation in your life should never precede or exceed God's mission. How effective are you in practicing "delayed gratification"? No matter what our income level, we will never achieve financial freedom until we are able to practice this discipline.

3. The most important thing we can do as a physical demonstration is to make a commitment. Follow through all the steps necessary for you to find financial freedom, and make a specific financial commitment to your faith community (storehouse) today.

Pray together in closing. Ask God to strengthen each one, to be present and powerful as steps towards financial freedom are taken, and to use this brief group study as a catalyst for what God will do in your church family. Consider saying this prayer aloud, from *Money Matters: Financial Freedom for All God's Children*:

Lord, we thank You again for Your persistent love and acceptance and Your patience in our lives. You are not one that deems that some people in this world should have more than others. You desire blessing for all of Your children, and Lord we want to be a part of that blessing. All around the world people are starving; they are starving physically and spiritually. They need to hear Your word to be liberated and we want to be a part of what You are going to do. So, Lord, right now we discern Your will and Your word to do what You are blessing. In the name of Jesus we pray, amen.

Appendix

The following items can assist a congregation when implementing Money Matters as a stewardship program into the *annual* life-cycle of a congregation. Most congregations reach a climax with stewardship strategies in the Fall, before Thanksgiving (which is timed with accepting pledges for giving in the new calendar year), yet a small number of churches are reaching the annual pledge stage in the Spring of the year, before Easter, when we celebrate the Cross and Resurrection. The annual timeline can easily be adjusted for churches that pledge in the Spring.* The following items are listed in the order that is found on the first item, an annual stewardship timeline.

1. Chief Stewardship Officer Annual Timeline

2. Kingdom Investor Hors d'oeuvres Initial Invitation

3. Kingdom Investor Dinner Invitation and RSVP

4. Kingdom Investor Invitation to Staff and RSVP

5. Kingdom Investor Invitation to Leadership Board Members

6. Annual Kingdom Investor Report: Hors d'oeuvres and Dinner

7. Board Member Follow-up Phone Call Script to Top Givers

8. Letter to All Active Givers

9. Commitment Card

10. Letter to Active Givers That Did Not Return Commitment Card

11. Monthly Mission Update Letter

12. Monthly Kingdom Investor Letter

*Source files with art are on the DVD. Source copy for all letters is on the DVD in a folder that can be opened, viewed, and downloaded on a computer with a DVD drive. The folder is named "Stewardship Resources." Also inside this folder is another folder containing full color images that you may use for projection in your stewardship classes, programs, and ministries. Please be an honorable and ethical steward: Avoid the temptation to e-mail or upload these images on the Internet.

1—CHIEF STEWARDSHIP OFFICER ANNUAL TIMELINE

A Seven-Week Process

Date	Communication	Content	Audience
Week 1			
Day 2	Letter to top givers	Invite to hors d'oeuvres	Givers > $10,000
Day 5	Letter to Kingdom Investors	Invite to dinner	Givers > $1,000
Day 5	Letter to all staff	Invite to dinner or hors d'oeuvre's	All staff
	All staff are expected to attend one of the events.		
Day 5	Letter to all Leadership Board	Attend all giver events if possible	All Board members
Days 5-6	Phone calls to top givers	Invite to hors d'oeuvres	Givers > $10,000
	Done by Leadership Board. This group is not asked to RSVP. RSVP's are taken over the phone.		
Week 2			
Day 8	Direct mail card goes out		
Week 3			
Day 15	Hors d'oeuvres event	Pastor shares message	Givers > $10,000
Day 16	Hors d'oeuvres event	Pastor shares message	Givers > $10,000
Week 4-5			
Days 19-23	Follow-up phone calls to top givers. Done by Leadership Board & Chief Stewardship Officer. Approximately ___ Investors who have not sent in an RSVP are called.	Invite to dinner	Givers > $1,000
Day 27-28	*First message on stewardship	Pastor	
Week 5			
Day 29	Dinner with Kingdom Investors	Pastor shares message	Givers > $1,000
Day 30	Dinner with Kingdom Investors	Pastor shares message	Givers > $1,000
Day 34-35	*Second message on stewardship	Pastor	
Week 6			
Day 41-42	*Third message on stewardship	Pastor	
Day 43	Letter to all active givers	Notify of commitment weekend	ALL givers
Week 7			
Day 48-49	*Commitment weekend (card)	Commitment card handed out in bulletin	Active giver-no card
Day 50	Letter to active givers - no card returned	Reminder	
		An Annual Cycle	
Monthly	Monthly Mission Update Letter	Examples of Mission	Givers < $1000
Monthly	Monthly Kingdom Investors Newsletter	Examples of Mission	Givers > $1,000
Spring	Picnics with Kingdom Investors	Pastor shares message	Givers > $1,000

*For all worship celebrations and message outlines, see Chapter 4.

2—KINGDOM INVESTOR HORS D'OEUVRES INVITATION

Day 2

Name _____

Address _____

City_____ State_____ Zip_____

Dear (first name):

MISSION: a calling, a purpose, a goal, an aim, an objective.

_____ Church is a faith community that is passionate about the MISSION of Jesus. As a Kingdom Investor, you are the key to this MISSION being fulfilled throughout 20xx and beyond. We all share an urgent desire to BRING, GROW, and SERVE. Your faithful tithes are the lifeblood that fuel this ministry.

You are cordially invited to enjoy hors d'oeuvres and conversation with Pastor _____ and the leadership team as the pastor updates us on the MISSION and future vision for _____Church, *where God grows hope, one life at a time.* We look forward to this time to be together with you!

When: Monday, Day 15   Where:

             Tuesday, Day 16   Where:

Time: 6:30 to 8:00 PM

We will be calling you next week to obtain your RSVP.

3—KINGDOM INVESTOR DINNER INVITATION

Day 5

Name _____

Address _____

City_____ State_____ Zip_____

Dear (first name):

MISSION! We are passionate about the mission of Jesus here at _____
_____Church. As a Kingdom Investor, you are the key to this mission being carried out in 20xx and beyond. We all share an urgent desire to **BRING ... GROW ... SERVE.** Your faithful tithes are the lifeblood that fuels this ministry.

> *"From everyone who has been given much, much will be demanded; and from the one who has been entrusted with much, much more will be asked* (Luke 12:48).

God has truly given us much and entrusted us with much. Nearly _____ persons each weekend call your church their spiritual home. That is an incredible trust God has given to us. As a Kingdom Investor, your part in carrying out this trust is vital. For you to do this, it is important to be informed.

In order to keep you informed, it is my pleasure to invite you to attend one of two identical gatherings. We will share a light meal and the current vision for mission. Please let us know which of the gathering times when we will be able to count on you:

Sunday, Day 28, 6:30 to 8:00 PM in the _____.
Monday, Day 29, 6:30 to 8:00 PM in the _____.

Childcare will be provided at the church. Please bring your children to the child-care wing. We will have servants available to direct you to the appropriate rooms. Your children will also be served a light meal.

Please complete the enclosed card and return it to us, so we can reserve a place for you.

On Mission with You,

Pastor _____

KINGDOM INVESTOR DINNER RSVP

NAME(S): (first and last names)

Please RSVP by Day 23 in one of the following ways:

    Return this reservation form to the church via **mail**.

    Return this reservation form to the church via the **offering plate**.

    Email your RSVP to chief stewardship officer.

    Phone in your RSVP to chief stewardship officer.

DATES:

_____ I will be attending the dinner on Day 28 at 6:30 PM.

    _____ # of adults attending

    _____ # of children (list ages)_____

_____ I will be attending the dinner on Day 29 at 6:30 PM.

    _____ # of adults attending

    _____ # of children (list ages)_____

- -

KEEP THIS PORTION FOR YOUR RECORDS

I will attend the Kingdom Investor Dinner on:

    _____ Sunday, Day 28 at 6:30 PM in the _____.

    _____ Monday, Day 29 at 6:30 PM in the _____.

(A donation to cover the cost of the meal will be collected at the dinners.)

4—KINGDOM INVESTOR DINNER INVITATION TO STAFF

Day 5

Name _____

Address _____

City_____ State_____ zip_____

Dear (first name):

MISSION! We are passionate about the mission of Jesus here at _____
_____ church. As a Kingdom Investor, you are the key to this
mission being carried out in 20xx and beyond. We all share an urgent desire
to **BRING ... GROW ... SERVE.** Your faithful tithes are the lifeblood that fuels
this ministry.

*"From everyone who has been given much, much will be demanded; and
from the one who has been entrusted with much, much more will be asked*
(Luke 12:48).

God has truly given us much and entrusted us with much. Nearly _____
persons each weekend call your church their spiritual home. This is an incredible trust that God has given to us.

As paid staff, we are all leaders of the church. Therefore, it is vitally important
for all of us to hear the message delivered to the Kingdom Investors. All staff
are expected to attend one of the two events listed below. Your spouse is
welcome to attend with you.

_____ Sunday, Day 28 at 6:30 PM in the _____.

_____ Monday, Day 29 at 6:30 PM in the _____.

Childcare will be provided. Please bring your children to the child-care room.
We will have servants available to direct you to the appropriate rooms. Your
children will also be served a light meal.

Please complete the enclosed card and return it to us so we can reserve a
place for you.

On Mission with You,

Pastor _____

KINGDOM INVESTOR DINNER RSVP

NAME(S): (first and last names)

Please RSVP by Day 23 in one of the following ways:

    Return this reservation form to the church via **mail**.

    Return this reservation form to the church via the **offering plate**.

    Email your RSVP to Chief Stewardship Officer.

    Phone in your RSVP to Chief Stewardship Officer.

DATES: _____

_____   I will be attending the dinner on (Sunday, Day 28) at 6:30 PM.

         _____ # of adults attending

         _____ # of children (list ages)_____

_____   I will be attending the dinner on Monday, Day 29 at 6:30 PM.
         _____ # of adults attending

         _____ # of children (list ages)_____

- -

KEEP THIS PORTION FOR YOUR RECORDS

I will attend the Kingdom Investor Dinner on:

     _____   Day 28 at 6:30 PM _____.

     _____   Day 29 at 6:30 PM _____.

(A donation to cover the cost of the meal will be collected at the dinners.)

5—KINGDOM INVESTOR INVITATION TO LEADERSHIP BOARD

Name _____

Address _____

City_____ State_____ Zip_____

Dear (first name):

MISSION: a calling, a purpose, a goal, an aim, an objective.

Together with you, we are passionate about the MISSION of Jesus here at _____Church. As a Kingdom Investor, you are the key to this MISSION being carried out in 20xx, and beyond. We all share an urgent desire to BRING, GROW, and SERVE, and your faithful tithes are the lifeblood that fuel the ministry.

As a Kingdom Investor and _____ Church leader, you are invited to attend the vision dinners described below. Your participation in all or as many of these events as possible is greatly appreciated.

Sincerely,

Chief Stewardship Officer

Hors D'oeuvres # 1   Hors D'oeuvres # 2

Day 15   Day 16

6:30 – 8:00 PM   6:30 – 8:00 PM

Location   Location

Dinner # 1   Dinner # 2

Day 28   Day 29

6:30 – 8:00 PM   6:30 – 8:00 PM

Location   Location

6—ANNUAL KINGDOM INVESTOR REPORT: HORS D'OEUVRES AND DINNER

Note how specifically ministry and mission are explained in this report at the Kingdom Investor meetings. Your numbers will be different, but you must have the numbers to show that the congregation's ministry is accountable and bearing fruit. God's people will give to implement a mission that has scope and significance, no matter what the church size, or the number of its programs or services.

Accomplishment of Annual Goals for Radical Hospitality, Passionate Worship, Faith-Forming Education and Experiences, and Risk-Taking Mission and Service

Radical Hospitality

This year we have continued to expand and develop our **"Value the Visitor"** initiative started last year, designed to create a welcoming atmosphere for all who attend. During this last calendar year, _____ **"Drop Bags"** filled with ministry information and welcome gifts were delivered to the front doors of all first-time visitors who live within a sixty-mile radius of the church.

In addition, we have held monthly **"Pizza with the Pastor"** sessions for newcomers to learn more about our church "DNA" and how to get connected. We developed and produced a new short video we now show at this event that features a visual tour of the key aspects of "Bring/Grow/Serve" throughout all ages of our ministries. More than _____ **individuals have attended** a "Pizza with the Pastor" session during the last 12 months to learn more about our church family.

Our summer **"tent events"** held on the front lawn are intended to create opportunities for hospitality and community every weekend all summer and into September. They attract new visitors from the community and also give our regular attenders key occasions to which they can invite their unchurched friends, family, and coworkers. This summer we held a tent event every weekend. The most popular tent events included a **June Father's Day Cruise-In** with nearly _____ **cars and vehicles** on display; the **July Blessing of the Bikes** for more than _____ **motorcyclists** (and hundreds of onlookers); **Blessing of the Backpacks** for _____ **preschool and school aged** children in August; and the **Community Festival in September** which featured inflatables, carnival rides, ministry display booths, music and food for _____ **of adults, teens, and children**.

We have moved forward with a variety of other steps, all intended to enhance the radical hospitality to which our congregation is committed:

The 12-year-old stained, well-worn carpet in the hallways and worship area was replaced, greatly increasing the appeal of these heavily-used spaces.

Our most strategic classroom was remodeled and redecorated to create a friendly atmosphere for "Pizza with the Pastor," as well as other events.

"CD" tables have been placed next to all exit doors on weekends, allowing attendees to conveniently purchase a CD of the weekend sermon message as they leave.

The traditional Wednesday night "food court" offered prior to Wednesday night classes every week was reinvented as the **"Wednesday Café"** with more economic prices, a more appealing food menu—and a new policy for **children ages 10 and under to eat free**. This children's meal policy has been hugely strategic for welcoming our newcomers and has increased meal attendance as well as class attendance on Wednesdays. During the last year we have served _____ **Wednesday night meals, including** _____ **free children's meals each week.**

Passionate Worship
We are excited to have accomplished our goal of launching a **new weekend worship celebration** for those in any kind of recovery, called our **"Next Step"** worship celebration at 7:15 PM, Saturday evenings. This new worship venue is led by a team of committed unpaid servants and has **grown to nearly** _____ **in attendance** every weekend. It is supported by a full complement of simultaneous children's activities in order to support parents who attend. This worship celebration is enhanced now by a new **Christian 12-Step** and a **new AA meeting** that both meet following. This allows the worship attendees to move into life-changing small group community that very evening every week.

A wonderful "passionate worship" event took place in July, when _____ **adults and children** were baptized (or reaffirmed their baptismal vows) at our **"Baptism on the Lawn"** celebration. Hundreds of family members and friends enjoyed a picnic lunch as they watched these believers take an incredible step of faith.

Other steps of progress made in passionate worship this year include:

The **complete replacement of our worship area sound system** with new equipment that has eliminated the loud, harsh quality of our worship music.

The addition of a **new part-time ministry internship position**. This person works with our worship design team, rehearses and leads the worship band and vocalists, and arranges all worship music each weekend.

The creation of a **new full-time staff position, children, and student music ministry specialist**. This person was hired and has already made great strides in worship contributions, including his support and leadership of our children's choirs, who sing in weekend worship (grade school Kidz on da Rock and the preschool Wee Kidz). This specialist has also already auditioned for and pulled together a middle school and a high school praise band, both of which will rotate leading opening worship on Wednesdays during the student ministry "Fusion/FastLane" event each week. New work in this area has also included creating a worship team of grade school students to help lead opening worship at the "Backyard" weekend children's class for third through fifth graders.

Faith-Forming Education and Experiences

We have surged forward this year with growth and progress for all ages in this area, featuring dozens of classes every week for every age and interest.

The third year of our establishment of the adult discipleship path, called the "**Core5**," has expanded into the children and student ministry class offerings—which now include age-appropriate Core5 courses on the same subjects. In addition, we have developed other new key spiritual education and learning experiences that have helped many grow in their faith and walk with God....

Our **cell group ministry** has deepened and grown during the last year, rapidly picking up momentum this fall. Our new adult cell group ministry director began at the end of March. His efforts have included instituting monthly cell group leader trainings, growing the attendance at our monthly "CellMatch" series within which people can connect into a cell group, expanding the weekly "Group Impact" discussion questions found in the worship bulletin into a cell group Bible study, updating our cell group records and establishing a strong connection throughout all the congregation.

Our efforts to help our staff grow spiritually as well as in their ministry skills have intensified during this year. The adult discipleship staff has completed two six-week sessions of in-house leadership/ministry skills training. Our childcare center teachers attend a monthly in-service to help hone their teacher skills, as well as a two-day training event held in August. Nearly our entire staff has completed "Ministry by Strengths" training in order to better maximize their talents within our strengths-based staff culture.

Risk-Taking Mission and Service

Our focus on mission continues locally, domestically, and around the world. Our "New Path" community ministries (food, car, furniture and support groups) are expanding. During the year we **assisted ____ persons through food, car, clothing, and furniture ministries**. The **food pantry** alone has provided for ____ **persons**.

Following are examples of abbreviated lists of all outreach camps, retreats, and mission trips completed this year.

FOR CHILDREN

Summer Camps

Kingdom Football Camp	__kids	__adults
Spirit Cheer Camp	__kids	__adults
Go! Camp	__kids	__adults
Summer children's outreach camp totals:	*__kids*	*__adults*

Family Mission Trips

January 31: New Path	__kids	__adults
February 26: Parkside	__kids	__adults
April 2: St. Patrick's Soup Kitchen	__kids	__adults
St. Francis Homeless Shelter	__kids	__adults

Children's Mission Trips

April 22-24: 6th grade Louisville	__kids	__teens
		__adults
April 8-9: 5th grade Columbus	__kids	__adults
Children's ministry mission trip totals:	__kids	__adults
Overall total for children's ministry:	*__kids*	*__adults*

FOR STUDENTS

Youth Mission Trips

New York: Dec. 1-5	__HS students	__adults
Detroit: Dec. 17-19	__HS students	__adults
Total for student mission trips:	*__students*	*__adults*

Retreats, Outreach Camps for Students

January MS Winter Retreat Ski Trip:	__MS students	__adults
March HS Ski Trip:	__MS students	__adults
Cornerstone Camp–June 29–July 4:	__HS students	__adults
Skate Camp–Aug. 5-7	__HS/MS students	__adults
Total for camps/outreach:	*__students*	*__adults*
Overall total for student ministry:	*__students*	*__servants (adult/teen)*

ADULT MISSION OUTREACH

Retreats, Outreach Camps for Students

Jamaica Medical Mission Trip:	__adults
Perkins Foundation, Jackson, MS:	__adults
Chicago, Illinois:	__adults
Nuevo Progresso Medical Mission:	__adults
Tijuana Christian Mission in July:	__adults
Tijuana Christian Mission in August:	__adults
Czech Republic English Camp:	__adults
New York, New York (November) registered:	__adults
Chicago, Illinois (December) registered:	__adults
Habitat for Humanity local projects:	__adults
Total for adult mission outreach:	*__adults*

GRAND TOTAL involved in mission through the church this year = _____. This represents a ____ percent increase in total number of people involved in mission through our church over last year!

Beyond the Local Church

Our church has expanded its risk-taking and service in additional new ways during the year:

Through our Sudan Christmas miracle offering we gave $ _____ in order to fund an agricultural project for five refugee camps in Darfur. We have worked to invite other churches across the country to join us as we look forward to our own Sudan Christmas miracle offering, aimed to help provide continued resources and education for the children of Sudan. In addition to giving sacrificially toward the Sudan, attendees also gave $ _____ for tsunami relief and $ _____ toward Hurricane Katrina relief. As with the Sudan project, these relief contributions were forwarded for deployment to the United Methodist Committee on Relief.

Looking Forward

Our deep hope is to keep pushing forward with the key, strategic initiatives that help our church family grow in spiritual maturity and engage in life-changing mission! We also look forward to continuing to make the ministry concepts and tools dreamed and deployed at our church available to other churches through conferences and resources so that they may grow along with us in advancing the mission of Jesus Christ.

7—BOARD MEMBER FOLLOW-UP
PHONE CALL SCRIPT TO TOP GIVERS

Calling points for dinners:

1. Pray.

2. Identify yourself as calling from _____ Church and your role as board member.

3. Explain that we are calling to make sure they had received the invitation to the Spring Kingdom Investor dinners.

4. Explain that the purpose of the dinner is to thank them for their faithful financial support, for the pastor to review the church's vision, and for the pastor to challenge us into the future. There will be a time allotted to ask questions of the pastor.

5. Take their RSVP over the phone. Record on the spreadsheet attached. We must know which night they are attending, the number of adults attending, the number of children attending, and the ages of the children.

6. Thank them again.

Calls need to be completed by Day 23. Forward the call information to (Chief Stewardship Officer's name and phone number or email address).

Day 28 at 6:30 PM in _____.

Day 29 at 6:30 PM in _____.

8—LETTER TO ALL ACTIVE GIVERS

Day 43

Name _____

Address _____

City_____ State_____ Zip_____

Dear (first and last names):

This month we have been learning about Devotion, Debt, & Discipline during our MONEY MATTERS series. God is definitely working among us, calling our hearts towards God's purposes. We've taken on a powerful challenge this month: to tithe all of our income, and to not increase our credit card debt in November. I am praying for your financial freedom, and anticipate greatly how this initiative will lead to financial freedom in many lives.

This coming weekend, Day 47-48 will culminate the series with our commitment weekend. Our Thanksgiving theme, "More Than Enough" explains God's math. When we practice God's biblical financial principles, there truly is "More Than Enough."

"Bring the whole tithe into the storehouse, that there may be food in my house. Test me in this," says the Lord *Almighty, "and see if I will not throw open the floodgates of heaven and pour out so much blessing that you will not have room enough for it."*—Malachi 3:10-11

It is because of YOUR faithful financial giving that thousands of lives are touched by the ministries of _____Church. Your continued giving is our life-blood to sustain the mission of Jesus.

I encourage you to prayerfully prepare to respond with your commitment to God during the worship celebrations Day 47-48. You will receive simple cards to write down your response at that time (a sample card appears on the back of this letter.) Also on the back of this letter is a snapshot of our current giving as a church, and a chart designed to help you plan your giving for the upcoming year.

Serving and giving alongside of you,

Pastor

—COMMITMENT CARD

source file for this card, in Adobe Photoshop and as an Adobe Acrobat
DF) file, can be found on the DVD that is packaged with this book. You may
odify it to fit the needs of your congregation.

**God can pour on the blessings
in astonishing ways**
so that you're **ready for anything** and everything.

2 Corinthians 9:8 (The Message)

MORE
THAN ENOUGH

giving period:
january 1 - december 31,_____

name:_____

address:_____

city, state, zip:_____

Phone:_____

OUR MISSION:

❏ YES! I will pray for our mission and ministry in this place. I estimate I will grow in my giving to the mission here at _____ Church next year as follows:

My yearly commitment to general funds and missions is $_____.
I plan to pay it as follows:

$_____Weekly $_____monthly
$_____quarterly $_____annually

❏ This represents an increase over what I am giving in $_____.

❏ I am interested in the automatic bank draft method of payment. (you will be contacted for specific information.)

❏ I Would like to receive my giving statements via E-mail. Please send my statement to:_____

I understand this estimate of giving may be
revised or cancelled at any time at my request.

10—LETTER TO ACTIVE GIVERS WHO DID NOT RETURN A COMMITMENT CARD

Day 43

Name _____

Address _____

City_____ State_____ Zip_____

Dear (first and last names):

Greetings in the name of Jesus!

During the worship celebrations on the weekend of Day 47-48, we celebrated God's amazing provision and concluded our Money Matters series by completing our commitment cards. Malachi 3:10 calls us to *bring the tithe to the "storehouse" that there may be resources for all God's children!* The cards are a tangible symbol of our trust in God's continued provision as we faithfully bring the tithe in 20xx.

In the event you were unable to join us that weekend, we understand you may still wish to complete a card. I have included one that you are invited to fill out and mail or bring to the church office. You may alternately complete an online card at _____(your church website)_____. We encourage you to prayerfully seek God's guidance as you make your own commitment for 20xx.

If you have already completed a commitment card, thank you for your faithfulness. There is no need to complete another card, and we apologize for any inconvenience.

Your faithful giving in 20xx has been what has allowed God's work through _____Church to move forward in powerful ways this year. We look forward to a great season of ministry together in 20xx.

Partnering with you in MISSION,
Chief Stewardship Officer

11—MONTHLY COMMUNICATION MISSION UPDATE LETTER

June 20xx

Name _____

Address _____

City_____ State_____ Zip_____

Dear (first name):

Spring and summer are times of great activity and the calendar tells me we aren't slowing down the mission here at _____ Church this summer either. Here is just a brief look at what is going on:

> Our Student Ministry has shifted into high gear. Mission trips are planned for this summer. A new weeknight Merge has begun, as well as new summer Bible studies for students under the tent.

> Our children are beginning to enjoy the first of the camps we've created. This year we are offering two camps for preschoolers as well!

> Adults are also hitting the mission trip trail. Trips to the Czech Republic, Kentucky, and Mississippi are just a few of the destinations.

> The tent is the weekend "happenin" place this summer. Each weekend a different event will be featured in the tent.

> Clubhouse is busy preparing their annual camping adventure. This year's theme is "Superheroes," with Jesus being the ultimate Superhero!

As you can see, summer is not a season of inactivity but a time to experience our greatest faith-ventures. Financially, we must continue to stay ON MISSION as well. It is imperative that we stay strong in this area in order for God to work through these and many other opportunities. *"To whom much is given, much will be required"* is our call to faithful stewardship.

My prayers on your behalf for a summer filled with Christ,
Chief Stewardship Officer

12—MONTHLY KINGDOM INVESTOR LETTER

In addition to the hors d'oeuvres and the dinner for Kingdom Investors in the Fall, the church continuously communicates the mission throughout the year. The Kingdom Investors are invited to Spring picnics, and a monthly newsletter is mailed to these core givers. An example follows:

August 20xx

Name _____

Address _____

City_____ State_____ Zip_____

Dear (first name):

Outreach: What exactly does this mean? The Merriam-Webster online dictionary provides the following definition:

out·reach/'aut-"rEch/*noun*
1 : the act of reaching out
2 : the extent or limit of reach <the *outreach* of the Ohio floods>
3 : the extending of services or assistance beyond current or usual limits <an *outreach* program>; *also* **:** the extent of such services or assistance

While all three definitions are correct, the third more closely hits what outreach means here at _____Church. An even better definition would be **MISSION DRIVEN.**

_____Church has a **MISSION DRIVEN** mindset. As the pastor stated in the message a few weeks ago, we are not just about singing songs and feeling good, we are about service. Here are just a few of the **MISSION DRIVEN** initiatives made possible by your faithfulness:

_____adults, students, and children were baptized or re-affirmed their baptism at our July 24th Baptism & Picnic on the Lawn.

On September 18th, we will again invite our neighbors to our Community Festival. This is an opportunity to invite hundreds of people onto our campus. This event is free, and our ministries are visible.

We are excited when God provides us the opportunity to share our ministries, resources and blessings with people who will experience *hope, one life at a time.* Thank you again for your faithful giving.

ON MISSION together with you,
Chief Stewardship Officer